Holy Cows and Hog Heaven

Holy Cows and Hog Heaven

The Food Buyer's Guide to
Farm Friendly Food

by
Joel Salatin

Polyface Inc.
Swoope, Virginia

Holy Cows and Hog Heaven, First Edition
Copyright © 2004 by Joel Salatin

Editing and book design by Jeff Ishee

About the cover: designed by Rachel Salatin, graphics by Keystrokes and Design

Library of Congress Control Number: 2004094248

ISBN: 0-9638109-4-4

Other books

by

Joel Salatin

Pastured Poultry Profit$
Salad Bar Beef
You Can Farm
Family Friendly Farming

All books available from:

Acres USA	1-800-355-5313
Amazon.com	www.amazon.com
Chelsea Green Publishing	1-800-311-2263
Stockman Grass Farmer	1-800-7489808

or by special order from your local bookstore.

Contents

Dedication

Although I have never dedicated any of my books to anyone in particular, this one I am dedicating to all the Polyface Farm patrons who have stood by us over the decades.

Joel

Acknowledgements

People consistently ask me: "When do you have time to write?" My reply: "In the winter when the snow flies." I am thankful we had enough bad weather this winter to drive me into the house and keep me at the desk long enough to finish this project.

Of course, my family and apprentices always pick up the slack when I'm writing. My wife Teresa intercepts phone calls and guards my time. Daughter Rachel, son and daughter-in-law Daniel and Sheri, and this time apprentice Galen Bontrager kept things running smoothly so I could plug away at the computer keyboard.

Our first grandson, Travis, has given me a renewed sense of continuity, sustainability, and how what I do today affects the world tomorrow.

In addition, I must acknowledge the worldview-shaping affect that my parents had when they risked everything and headed to Venezuela in the late 1940s to own and operate an environmentally-sensible farm. That experience, which included losing the farm during a period of political instability, helped shape my political views.

As a Christian libertarian environmentalist capitalist, I appreciate reading widely divergent material to create an eclectic base from which to formulate opinions. This is one reason why every political persuasion will find things to love and things to hate about this book. It's just where I am.

Finally, a deep thank you goes to Jeff Ishee, who makes all these words line up on camera ready copy.

FOREWORD

I didn't have much of a choice about meeting Joel Salatin.

I'd been working on an article about the cattle industry, when I heard about this farmer in Virginia who was raising terrific grass-finished beef. So I phoned him, identified myself as a writer for the New York Times Magazine, and after we'd chatted a bit about the horrors of industrial meat, I asked if I could try one of his steaks.

"Sure, come by the farm any time."

I explained that I lived in Connecticut, so maybe instead he could ship me a rib eye or two?

"Sorry, but we only sell locally."

I interpreted this to mean he wasn't set up for shipping, so I offered to give him my Fed Ex account number.

"No, I don't think you understand. We have a policy here of never shipping food more than fifty miles from the farm. I have a problem with Fed-Exing meat clear across the country. If you want to try one of our steaks, I'm afraid you're just going to have to come down to Swoope."

I realized then and there that Joel Salatin was a man dead serious about his principles, and that there was no principle as dear to him as local food. Local trumped a host of other good words about food, including organic, sustainable, free-range, humanely raised, pesticide-free, whatever.

If we are really serious about overturning our industrial food chain, he believes, we have to start by turning our backs on Wal-Mart and Federal Express, and buying directly from farmers we trusted. What's more, we cannot delegate the crucial work of determining which farmers deserved our trust, not to the USDA, not to certifiers, not even to writers from the New York Times. Buy "farm friendly food" from local people you trust, and almost all the problems of the industrial food system – its unconscionable cost in energy, public health, environmental degradation, and the deterioration of work and community—will pretty much take care of themselves. That at least is Joel Salatin's message in Holy Cows and Hog Heaven, the manifesto you hold in your hands.

Why should local –rather than, say, organic-- be the linchpin to this revolution? Because a farmer dependant on a local market is far more likely to raise a variety of crops, rather than specialize in the one or two plants or animals that the national market demands. That system wants all its apples from Washington State, all its lettuce from California (and make that Iceberg, please), and its corn from Iowa. Well it turns out the people who live in Iowa can only eat so much corn and soybeans; if Iowans were eating locally, rather than from the supermarket, their farmers would soon learn how to grow a few other things besides. And as soon as they gave up on their monocultures of corn and soy, they would quickly discover they could also give up on their pesticides and chemical fertilizers, because a diversified farm will produce its own fertility and its own pest control.

Almost all of the problems of our industrial food system flow from the original sin of monoculture. Monoculture may be a powerful industrial idea –it produces economies of scale and all sorts of other efficiencies— but it runs diametrically counter to the way nature works, which nothing in this world can do indefinitely. Insect resistance, agricultural pollution, food-borne illness, and antibiotic resistance are what happen when the logic of monoculture runs up against the logic of nature. Monoculture can't survive this encounter without one industrial Band-Aid after another—beginning with chemicals and ending (well, one can hope) with genetically modified crops and irradiation. The answer to the problems of monoculture is polyculture, and, to get back to where we started, the way to support polyculture is by buying food from local farms that practice it.

Eventually I made it down to Swoope to score my steak and visit Polyface Farm. This was like no other farm I'd ever set foot on —indeed, to call it a farm scarcely does justice to the intricate dance of species that Joel Salatin is choreographing on his 500 beautiful acres. I found not only cattle but also chickens and pigs, rabbits and sheep and turkeys participating in a dance of symbiosis that unfolded on a verdant stage of grass. In fact if you ask him, Joel will tell you he's not a cattle rancher or a chicken farmer but a "grass farmer," for the whole enterprise depends on the diminutive polyculture of plants and animals resident in every square foot of pasture - the fescues and clovers and earthworms that make the meals for the cattle which in turn feed the chickens and pigs which in turn feed the pastures that feed the cattle.

Joel will tell you that his most profitable crop is his chicken – more broilers and eggs! is what the marketplace is loudly telling him to do. But if Joel were to listen to the siren song of monoculture, were he to get into chickens big time, the whole self-sustaining system that is Polyface Farm would swiftly break down. The pastures can only absorb so much chicken manure, and if the chickens no longer got to dine on the fat grubs in the cow patties, their eggs and meat would no longer taste as good as they do. Everything's connected, and everything depends on finding its proper scale.

Joel's deep understanding and practice of these principles are why he is one of the most creative, productive and sustainable farmers working in America today. He is also one of the most influential farmers in America, because he can explain with unusual clarity (and even humor) how these principles connect to other principles — how decisions about the way we eat determines not only the biology in a square foot of pasture, but also whether or not that square foot of planet earth will remain in pasture or succumb to suburban lawn or driveway asphalt. For conservation is another compelling argument for local food: it is the surest way to preserve the rural landscape we profess to love but that, meal by meal, bite by bite, we are dooming. Suburban sprawl is about how we eat too. It's all connected.

What I think is most important about Joel's farming and his writing is that he not only makes those vital connections vivid, but gives us non-farmers –the eaters of the world-- a sense of our awesome power to do something about them. His message is that we eaters can change the world, one meal at a time.

I don't know about you, but I've always hated thinking of myself as "a consumer." What a dumb beast that character is, looking out for number one, prowling the supermarket aisle for the best deal, using up the world to gratify his desires. So much in modern life conspires to make this character our primary identity, reducing us to homo consumericus. I'm not just talking about the advertisers and marketers, who encourage us to define ourselves by the car we drive, but even the President, who tells us the best way we can help our country in these troubled times is to go down to the mall and keep on shopping.

With this book, Joel Salatin proposes a radically different vision of what it means to be a consumer, one that brims with hope and possibility and power. His proposition is that we consumers are in fact creators, and that our simplest everyday food-buying decisions represent one of the most important and influential votes we can cast. Shop at Wal-Mart or McDonald's and you support an industrial food chain that connects you to a monoculture of corn somewhere in Iowa, not to mention to Monsanto and Dupont, the dead zone in the Gulf of Mexico, and arguably even the war in the other Gulf. It's all connected.

There's a lot about modern civilization we may be powerless to change, but the food system is different: it is uniquely sensitive to our buying decisions. You can make a very different choice, choose to connect to something else: to that square foot of pasture in the farm down the road, to the grass that feeds the cattle that feeds the chickens that feed you and, by the way, taste so incredibly good. That's another thing about food that is different: It turns out we can have our cake and eat it too, for the right food choice – the most ethical, the most humane, the most sustainable–– happens also to be the freshest and tastiest.

Who ever said there's no free lunch?

Michael Pollen - July 2004

INTRODUCTION

Farm subsidies. Farmland preservation. Food-borne illness. Antibiotic resistance. Genetic engineering. Clones. Corporate power. Globalism. Biosecurity. Factory farms. Chemical use. Healthy food. Organic certification.

After discussing any one of these issues, our tendency is to ask, almost rhetorically because we really can't believe there's an answer: "So what can I do?"

Every day you and I decide what will be on our dinner plate. It's a decision for which we can accept responsibility, or one that we can take a defeatist attitude and sigh: "What's the use?"

All of us need to be empowered. In the face of global and cultural issues seemingly spinning out of control and too big to tackle, you and I can dramatically influence our world. The wheels of legislation turn slowly. Megapolitical trends are a long time developing and a long time changing.

But you and I do not need to wait for societal trends to catch up with us. I am a fulltime Christian libertarian capitalist environmentalist farmer who supplies families and restaurants with beyond organic food in Virginia's Shenandoah Valley. Every day I have conversations with people who want to know:

- Why can't I get your wonderful food in the supermarket?
- Do you ship?
- Why does your food taste so much better than what's in the store?
- Why is your food so clean?
- I like what you have now, but can you produce more variety and more volume?
- Can you handle more customers?
- What can I do to help you?
- Are you having any problems with the government?
- Why are your prices higher than in the store?
- Why can't I get eggs from you in November?
- Why don't you do boneless, skinless, breast?
- Everything is so healthy and beautiful here, why don't more people farm this way?
- How can I get my friends and neighbors to eat this kind of food?
- Do you have information that I can use to convince people not to buy all their food at the conventional supermarket?
- I have a cousin in Indiana. How can she get this kind of food?
- How did the corporations get all this power?
- Are other people doing this kind of farming?

The questions are endless, and they're all sincere, meaningful, and insightful. I spend hours explaining why we farm the way we farm, how it heals the world, and how people can be a part of this growing farm friendly food movement.

The current food system in the United States is not farm friendly. What good is a farm without a farmer? A farmscape without its farmers is like a classroom without students. Trying to compensate for this epic loss is costing society huge amounts of money, both private and public. From conservation easements to development rights to beginning farmer programs, our culture is waking up to the fact that a nation without productive farmland and the farmers who care for it is a sick, vulnerable nation.

Coupled with this is growing disenfranchisement with corporate centralization, consolidation, and amalgamation within the food industry. From beef cattle to carrots, the food is controlled by just a handful of powerful interests. All sorts of policy wonks have different opinions about how to deal with these issues. From Country Of Origin Labeling (COOL) to enforcement of anti-trust laws, grassroots efforts are fighting back against a food system that appears to be:

- Squeezing profit margins tighter and tighter, running more farmers out of business.
- Introducing more questionable practices like irradiation and genetic engineering.
- Fraternizing more cozily between regulators and private corporations.
- Less and less responsive to nutrition.
- Destroying the landscape with more mono-cropping and overgrazing.
- Polluting the air and water with more Concentrated Animal Feeding Operations (CAFOs).

These efforts require fundraising, mass mailings, executive directors, office space, and countless hours of both paid and donated labor. They also involve costly travel to public hearings, reams of newsprint, advertisements, and countless media interviews. Often they factionalize their constituencies, creating in-fighting and lost motion. Much of this work is important and needful. I applaud these efforts.

But with all deference to these efforts, I humbly submit that a more efficient way exists to get where we want to go. At least for those of us who do not worship at the altar of globalism and Wall Street.

I suggest that you and I can make a difference, right now, right here, today. We do not need to join an organization, as important as that may be, to effect the changes we want to see. We can join the growing alternative, opt-out movement with our food purchases.

Thousands of farmers are as concerned about these issues as are informed, caring, savvy food buyers. These farmers and their farms, which come in all shapes and sizes, are producing clean, environmentally-enhancing food and fiber outside the conventional paradigms. Some are certified organic. Some are beyond organic. Some are biodynamic.

But the common threads that unite them are:
- a love for the land.
- a respect for nature's design.
- a discerning spirit toward alleged technological panaceas.
- a distrust of global agendas.
- a skepticism toward conventional commodity wholesale marketing.
- a yearning to shorten the distance between producer and buyer.
- a deep sense of ecological ethics and community responsibility.

While this movement is partly about healthier, more nutritious food, it is fundamentally about food that maintains and regenerates farms and the farmers who caretake them. You and I, in the food choices we make, can move this system toward the one we want to see, or a system of industrial fecal factory fare.

Not one of us can escape the responsibility for making this decision. We can elect to not have a driver's license and thereby escape making decisions about roads. We can decide not to have electricity and throw the TV in the dumpster and not have to hassle with our families over what to watch.

But neither you nor I, nor anybody else, can opt out of the food system. We're in it. We're stuck. We can make excuses about availability and price. We can make excuses about time and money. We can cry over fairness and ignorance. But in the final analysis, we can do something. Whether it's sprouting mung beans in a jar or starting a buying club serviced directly by a farmer, we can do things today that will move our food system toward or away from farm friendly food.

Farm friendly food is good for our landscapes, our bodies, homeland security, and every other thing that is good and noble. Thousands of farmers view their production as a sacred trust between their land and the dinner plate. Those who take such a view should be patronized. They should be encouraged. You and I should buy their food.

To move this effort forward, I have endeavored to inform you, the food buyer, about the farmers' world and your responsibility in it. All of us who produce farm friendly food want to connect more intimately with our patrons in order to deepen mutual appreciation and loyalty. It's all about me entering your world and you entering mine. It's all about mutual love, honor, and respect. My prayer is that this book will do just that. Enjoy.

Joel Salatin
Summer, 2004

The Farm Friendly Producer

Chapter 1

Trustworthy to Maintain Consistency

P roducer integrity is the foundation of farm friendly food. Integrity cannot be legislated, certified, formulated or placed on a spreadsheet. The temptation to cut corners is as real in adulthood as it is in infancy.

Doing just what is necessary to get by is like an attitudinal cancer. It is the number one complaint of every employer in the culture. Show me a dishwasher who really cares how the plates come out, who does a great job for the sheer integrity of doing a great job, and I'll show you a dishwasher who will be assistant manager in six months at any restaurant in the country.

What construction foreman doesn't notice a Johnny-on-the-spot concrete toter who gets his wheelbarrow where it's needed when it's needed without having to be prodded? What building crew, when given a half hour for lunch, jumps back to the job at 29 minutes? Normally if a guy returns to work at 35 minutes, the rest of the crew gives him the raspberries, taunting him as some sort of brown-noser or goody-two-shoes.

The propensity to cut corners is probably the defining difference between a run-of-the-mill worker and a craftsman, or artisan. Watch an artisinal potter work a lump of clay and it's sheer poetry. The skill, care, and technique come together to yield exquisite form and function. What artisinal potter would put shoddy material on the "For Sale" shelf?

2

Trustworthy to Maintain Consistency

All of us appreciate these principles in our daily lives. Teachers know who the deadbeats are in the school. Telephone operators know whose cubicle exudes customer helpfulness and whose radiates haughtiness, shortness, and bureaucratic gobbleydegook. Integrity in the workplace is something all of us can spot. We all know the differences are there.

Often cutting corners and slipshod work can be hidden for awhile. Fraudulent accounting at Enron created an unprecedented collapse, and further fueled the distrust of everything big. Insider trading and corruption, when they reach the halls of Congress or Blue Chip corporations, erode public trust. Sexual scandals, smoke-filled rooms, wheeling and dealing are all symptomatic of untrustworthiness and a lack of integrity.

Are the stewards of our food system immune to these temptations? Are farmers immune? Of course not. The best remedy for these temptations is accountability. And a food system in which the average morsel travels 1,500 miles between farm and plate is guaranteed to have very little accountability.

What kind of a producer are you willing to trust with your food? What kind of a system are you willing to trust with your food? How do you know you have a trustworthy farmer and not an opportunist wanting to cash in on the clean, local, enviro-friendly market? Every life sector has its honorables and its charlatans.

And no more than putting a backwards collar on a man makes him honest--how many clergymen have run off with their secretaries?-- neither does using the word "organic" or "local" make a farmer honest. Every new opportunity attracts shysters, and the organic community sure has a pile of them, certified or not.

At the risk of being offensive, especially to my conventional farmer friends, let me point out that America's food system rewards lack of integrity. From the farmers who feed fermented forages and grain to herbivores in direct opposition to nature's template, to bovine ionophore hormone implants to make steers grow faster, the entire food system is predicated on shortcutting honesty. No one should have needed the reality of mad cow and the millions of taxpayer supported studies in sophisticated laboratories conducted by legions of academic geeks to

3

make us understand that feeding chicken guts and cow brains to herbivores may not be a good idea.

For too long the food system has rewarded producers who flaunt human cleverness in the face of nature and believe human arrogance can trump nature's principles forever. Nature bats last, and the food system is crying out for changes. These cries can be heard in the multitude of new Latin words all of us have learned to say: camphylobacter, salmonella, lysteria, E. coli. Why can't farmers hear these cries?

One reason is that listening to them is not masculine. Please humor me a bit of sexist stereotyping. How many fathers, when our infant child awakes crying in the night, lie still hoping our wives will think we're asleep and get up to tend the little tyke so we can go on snoozing? Who takes the children to the pediatrician? Mom, not Dad. Who strokes the feverish forehead of a child? Mom, not Dad.

Men and women are different, and this feminine nurturing spirit keys into the intuitive nature of the fairer sex. I have talked to hundreds of groups about clean food production, and I will take a 15-member garden club over a 100-member Ruritan Club any time of the day. Why? When I start talking about caring for plants and animals, growing food as God intended, women are right with me. They know about sniffles and cheek color and countenance.

We men are too busy getting smelly and greasy, enjoying the thunder of pig iron under our thighs, to hear nature's voice. It's just not masculine for the farmer to come in and tell his loving Matilda that he spent the day making the cows happy. It's just not masculine to be energized by happy chickens. And yet it is that quality that creates the conscience necessary to raise food with integrity. If a farmer is not more jazzed over happy chickens than he is over the volume, the structure, the profit--he's not a trustworthy farmer. And yet in our culture's food system, can you find one USDA bulletin, one corporate directive, one industry checkoff bulletin, one Super Bowl advertisement, that dares to ask: "Did the eggs come from happy chickens? Did the tomatoes come from happy plants?"

As a buyer of honest food, you must determine if your farmer is trustworthy. That is where it all starts. Here is a checklist that might help:

Trustworthy to Maintain Consistency

- Look at his bookshelf. What is he reading? I am much more interested in a farmers' books than whether he is government organic certified. Anyone can adopt a set of lingo to join the latest marketing fad; but a farmer who truly seeks a different approach will immerse himself in the literature on that subject. If his magazine rack is loaded with conventional fare, beware. Is he reading the stuff you like? Is what he is feeding his mind and soul consistent with your beliefs?

- What do his business peers say? Virtually every state has an alternative food system support group. They use different buzzwords to delineate their bent: sustainable, organic, ecological, stewardship, biological, practical. Is your farmer affiliated with these groups and what do they say? A quick phone call is all you'll need. Just as teachers in any school know who the slouches are, and the doctors in any hospital know who the golddiggers are, peers in the clean farming business will know the scuttlebutt. These are fairly closeknit fraternities due to the camaraderie that naturally develops in an underdog group. Ask around to find out if your farmer is true blue.

- What do his neighbors say? Again, with more prisoners in our country than farmers, farmers have become a virtual subculture. If you don't believe it, attend the next auction at the local livestock sale barn. If you don't feel like the ugly duckling, my name's not Joel Salatin. Reputable farmers are respected by their neighbors. Oh, certainly the neighbors may think them weird, or odd, or even hobbyists. But trustworthy farmers earn their place in their community. If your sleuthing turns up statements like "He never pays his bills" or "His weeds replant the whole county" or "His cows are always in the road" or "He gets monthly visits from the Immigration and Naturalization Service," you may want to do some further checking. The people who live closest to you tend to have a pretty good idea about what is going on.

- Visit the farm. The proof is in the pudding. What does it look like? Does he have to apologize for everything? Certainly things happen. Snows break down shed roofs. Droughts turn fields brown. Every day is not picture perfect. But do you get an overall impression of order, effort, happiness, and health? Is it a place you would like to live? Is it a place that leaves you

5

refreshed and energized? A farmer is a landscape sculptor. How does his landscape look compared to what is across the boundary fence? In any given season, this will often be one of the most dramatic signals of true stewardship.

Above all, do not be afraid to subject your farmer to the same level of scrutiny that you would your auto mechanic, your pediatrician, or your babysitter. How many of us make judgment calls based on first impressions or a bit of basic questioning? As a culture, we've been taught that this is responsible buyer behavior in every sector of business except in the food sector. In that sector, we are supposed to blindly believe every public relations statement issued by the government or industry and not question.

"We have the safest food in the world" follows every single pathogen scare, every discovery of mad cow, every outbreak of hepatitis and every food recall. It's like saying "Amen" at the end of the prayer. No matter how incriminating, no matter how obviously malfunctioning, no matter how debilitating the announcement, "we have the safest food in the world" is supposed to make the booboo all better.

As a responsible food buyer who wants to patronize farm friendly fare, you must be courageous and responsible enough to question. You must know to your own satisfaction that the farmer you patronize can be trusted. Once you've established trust, other factors enter into the food conversation. Those additional aspects will be discussed in the next three chapters. But they cannot even enter into the discussion until you know that you can trust what is said. Being able to trust in a conversation is at once empowering and liberating. Trustworthy producers are the only ones who are truly farm friendly.

Chapter 2

Committed to Appropriate Size

"Why don't you become the Frank Perdue of pastured poultry?" The question came from an entrepreneurial visitor who stopped by to see the farm and realized the marketing possibilities of our pastured chicken.

Another entrepreneur friend stopped by and promised me a six figure income if I'd join up with his other two associates in a pastured poultry venture that would utilize cheap foreign labor to move shelters and process birds while a fleet of refrigerated trucks delivered chickens up and down the eastern seaboard.

The problem with both of these offers is one of scale. Just because a prototype works does not mean that exponentially increasing its size guarantees identical success. We've seen this principle even in the industrial world. Who would have thought when the sleek, droop-nosed embodiment of techno-glitzy new millennium air travel, the Concorde Supersonic Transport, made its first landing at Kennedy International Airport that in merely two decades, it would be obsolete?

Oh, certainly most of us would have agreed that it would be obsolete, but we would have envisioned replacement by a bigger, faster, more luxurious machine. Instead, it was simply obsolete compared to the stodgy 747. As they say, who would have thunk?

Committed to Appropriate Size

A study of paradigms reveals that every paradigm exceeds its point of efficiency before being replaced by the new paradigm. The pendulum of development and discovery never hangs perfectly in the middle; it's always to one side. And in order to come back to the middle, it has to go a little too far to one side first. That is why every mature paradigm, is it becomes inefficient and dysfunctional, creates the opportunity for the replacement paradigm.

An elephant is its appropriate size to be a successful elephant. A mouse is likewise a successful mouse because of its size. An elephant the size of a mouse would not be a very successful elephant, and a mouse the size of an elephant would not be a very successful mouse. Form and function go hand in hand to define appropriate scale.

My impression of the industrial food system today is that the most perfect dairy for the country would be one huge cow centrally located in the grain belt, maybe in Nebraska, with a web of megapipes carrying milk from a county-sized udder to every city. The mouth would be the size of a Wal-Mart Supercenter, ingesting food a train car load at a time. The greatest wonder of this cow would be its ingenious and astronomical colostomy that would duct all the manure away in a 20-foot diameter pipe. Any agriculture economics student in the country worth his salt could develop a computer spreadsheet showing the efficiency and should-have rationale of such a critter. In typical cow college fashion, however, this alleged efficiency would not measure input costs like petroleum, environmental footprints, milk quality, bovine happiness, and effluent utilization. Only a couple of variables would be plugged in and voila, the monster cow would be the ideal of the land. Nature has a way of weeding out the freaks. In spite of all modern science can do, and in spite of all the computer programs at our disposal, the Creator's design eventually surfaces as the most efficient, and the most appropriate.

The cattle industry went through a 40-year phase promoting bigger physiques. Blue ribbons were awarded on how high the hips were off the floor. A friend of mine attended a beef symposium and toward the end asked one of the professors: "What can we do to make the beef better?"

The professor got this quizzical look on his face and asked: "You mean, how can we grow it faster?"

My friend replied: "No, I mean make it better."

9

Holy Cows and Hog Heaven

The befuddled professor, not to be outdone, queried again: "You mean, how can we make it bigger?"

My frustrated friend clarified: "No, I mean make it better."

In total bewilderment and incredulity, the professor asked: "Why would you want to do that?"

Unfortunately, that is normative in America's food system. No one is asking what makes food better or how to produce food on farms that are ecological and economic profit centers for their communities. The only consideration is how to grow it faster, cheaper, and bigger.

I questioned this axiom of our modern food system to a visiting agricultural historian from the Smithsonian at a symposium. His response was that bigger is always better. Our culture, he said, was predicated on a bigger fort that was more likely to withstand attack. A bigger cannon was more likely to knock out the enemy. And by extension, a bigger turkey will make us a better country. Talk about a leap of faith. The military industrial complex sitting squarely on the Thanksgiving table. Makes you proud.

The reason I quickly turned down both of those glittery offers from pastured poultry empire-builder entrepreneurs was because our farm receives a certain amount of sunshine, a certain amount of rain, and is only one little component of a larger ecosystem. Let me be very practical. We cover one acre with each 500 pastured broilers that we grow. We move them daily in portable, floorless shelters across the pasture. Their droppings are putting on 200 pounds of nitrogen per acre at this 500-bird rate. In our bioregion, a lush, healthy, fully utilized pasture can only uptake and metabolize about 300 pounds of nitrogen per year.

That is why we try not to cover any square foot twice in one year with the broilers, because a second coverage would automatically put us into the 400-pound nitrogen range and the extra 100 pounds would either vaporize into the air or leach into the groundwater and become a contaminant. Even pastured poultry can become an ecological liability. Amazingly, when we compute the land necessary to grow the grain for 500 broilers, it comes out to one acre. The point being that when we look at the whole and define the parameters from an entire ecosystem standpoint, it all balances out.

Compare that to the vertically integrated poultry industry, which for decades has been feeding its manure to cattle because it simply cannot dispose of it fast enough. For some reason, cows have always become the garbage cans for industrial wastes. The same is true of confinement dairy farms in California that burn the manure in electric power plants. The inappropriate scale turns nature's magic soil elixir into toxic waste. That is a tragedy of epic proportions. And immoral to boot.

A farm friendly producer does not bury his community in excrement and toxicity in order to grow government-subsidized food for someplace halfway around the world. Neither does a farm friendly producer bury his community in foreigners who overload the school system, overload the social services, and overload the courts. A food system that cannot hire its neighbors is exhibiting characteristics of an empire. An empire has no soul, no conscience, no boundaries. It simply wants to take, to grow, to conquer.

I'd like to ask the president of a poultry corporation: "How many confinement chicken houses are enough?" I believe the answer would be the one J. Paul Getty allegedly gave when asked: "How much money is enough?"

He is reported to have responded: "One more dollar." Once the chicken farms have polluted the groundwater, upset the local social culture, stunk up the air, and adulterated the school system, is there no shame, no conscience, no responsibility? No, just one more house. One more house. One more house. One more house. One more house.

Farm friendly producers understand that their lives are bounded by environmental, emotional, and economic factors. Override those natural constraints, and farms become liabilities rather than assets. They become places nobody wants to visit. They become devoid of vibrant farmers, operated instead by feudal serfs locked into a multinational corporate Wall Street agenda without morals or ethics.

The world is full of bad big businesses that grew up from good small businesses. Farm friendly producers are committed to appropriate scale. They are not empire builders. "As a man thinks in his heart, so is

11

he" is not just Biblically accurate, it is experientially corroborated every day.

Any small farmer who aspires to an empire is no different than any multinational corporate entity. He has already made the mental leap, the value compromise, to be there. The fact that he has not yet arrived does not mitigate how such a goal will be expressed in the food he produces. The food produced is merely an extension of the farmer's mindset. Here are some red flags to watch for in determining if your producer has an empire mentality:

- Single product focus. Because every new product requires its own special infrastructure and knowledge base, the temptation is to produce more and more of the same thing rather than diversify to other products. Growing more of the same inevitably bumps biological boundaries. Diversifying the product mix allows the producer to grow the business without compromising product or environmental integrity.

- Trademarks and copyrights. Protectionism indicates a fear of competition, and anyone who fears competition is not confident in their own product integrity. I have purposely not trademarked terms I've invented like "Pastured Poultry" or "Salad Bar Beef" or "Eggmobiles" or "Pigaerators" simply because I'd like to see them be the language of the land. Furthermore, I trust my customers and my products enough, and believe in our models enough, to believe there is plenty to go around. In the words of Stephen Covey, *plenty instead of scarcity*. Turf wars are the inevitable result of an empire mentality.

- Terminology like "market share" and "economies of scale". Certainly these are real terms, but when a producer seeks to garner a certain percentage of market share as a goal, he will inherently cut corners to get there. The corners cut may not necessarily be in product integrity; it may simply be using "dog eat dog" business tactics to drive a competitor out of business. The whole point of farm friendly food is that the landscape is dotted with many and varied farms, not one big centralized one gobbling up the neighbors. Think of it as teacher/pupil ratio. A great teacher does not become more effective by consolidating classrooms and having her teach 100 students instead of 30. She is most effective when she inspires other teachers to do better with their 30. Natural reproduction is through duplication, not annihilation.

- Fancy packaging. Glitzy packaging comes at a huge price, and the volume required to justify the cost invariably means large scale production. This doesn't mean that a farmer should never use his logo or address on products. But I've seen many egg cartons, for example, that cost a quarter apiece--see-through trifolds with four-color separation on the label. The tractor-trailer load volumes necessary to customize those glitzy cartons mandate a volume that, if it hasn't already, will eventually lead the farmer down the slippery slope of empire building. Farm friendly producers invest in their production quality, not fancy packaging.

- Autonomy among collaborators. Many larger organic outfits have a no-sell contract with growers, so that even if a neighbor comes to the farm to buy a carrot, the producer is prohibited from selling her one. All of her carrots must go to the company store. This is similar to the contracts the vertically integrated poultry industry makes its growers sign: they cannot even raise one egg for their household use. They can't raise a turkey for the neighbor or some broilers on the back forty for the church barbecue. Empire builders love to deprive their grower networks of the freedom to do some freelance production and marketing.

- Aspiring to sell through Wal-Mart. I wish I had a nickel for every time I've been asked: "Can I get your stuff at the supermarket?" The truth about supermarkets is that they serve a very important function: moving lots of stuff long distances cheaply. Supermarkets, organic or otherwise, do not do a good job of creating food connections, maintaining integrity, or especially insuring that farmers get a living wage. Supermarkets are predicated on pitting all their suppliers against each other on price, paying their vendors up to 90 days after product delivery (this finances the store on the vendors' money), and carrying no loyalty to local producers who must deal with seasonality and cash flow. When it's all said and done, nothing is more efficient than a community feeding itself. And yet you can walk into any Wal-Mart in the country and find hardly an item that was produced within 100 miles of that store. Except for a few notable locally controlled exceptions, supermarkets cater to the

13

empire builders. And any producer who aspires to sell there is starstruck, not customer struck.

Chapter 3

Neighbor Friendly

T he industrial food system has created an agriculture that is smelly, noisy, dusty, and ugly. Travel by a 100,000 head cattle feedlot in Colorado or Nebraska and tell me that's where you want to go for a picnic. Visit a sweet corn farm during its weekly pesticide application and turn your children loose to pick wildflowers among the workers sporting the latest moonsuit hazard wear.

Nuisance suits against farmers have become so common that legislatures around the country have passed "Right to Farm" laws. I call these "Right to Stink up the Neighborhood Laws." The notion that farms by definition must be unfriendly to neighbors is a recent invention of the industrial empire production system.

The bucolic meadow romps of yesteryear have been replaced with "No Trespassing: Biosecurity" signs at farmgates all across the fruited plain. Only designated "Agritainment" farms allow visits, and their success simply illustrates the dearth of urban-rural interaction in our current culture.

The most unfortunate result of this neighbor unfriendliness is the steady passage of regulations that put farmers out of business. And clean farmers get sucked up in the bureaucratic malaise as well as the improprietous ones. Bureaucrats make no distinction between small and large, clean and unclean, neighbor friendly or neighbor unfriendly. Because of what they have become in the centralized, amalgamated, industrial model, abattoirs are prohibited in virtually every agricultural zone in the country. Nobody wants to live next to a 100,000 square foot slaughterhouse.

But what about a farmer processing a few chickens one day a week for customers who come from the community and want to purchase something outside Wal-Mart fare? In most agricultural districts, woodworking businesses are prohibited. Again, the dust, noise, and size of the normal ones make a nasty neighbor. But what about an artisinal cabinetmaker working by himself with maybe one employee, building a dozen pieces of furniture a year and repairing broken pieces for community customers? Doesn't matter the size--it's still woodworking. I ask you: "What better place to locate a woodworking shop than near the woods?"

Here in our area, our pastured poultry is considered a bioterrorist threat to the industry because Red Winged Blackbirds, Starlings, and Sparrows commune with our chickens and supposedly spread their diseases to their industrial cousins. Never mind that we have not had one outbreak of disease in 40 years. Never mind that the fecal factory inhumane concentration camp birds are living in sewage air and sleeping on dung. Never mind that industrial birds have poor immune systems caused in part by respiratory mucous membrane lesions from breathing in fecal particulate air.

A packing house for a Community Supported Agriculture farm is completely different than one for Jolly Green Giant, but to the regulators, a packing house is a packing house. I do not know how we can get sanity back into these regulations, and that is not the point of this discussion. But the food system--and especially farmers--have done this to ourselves by arrogantly throwing in our neighbors' faces phrases like "Property Rights" and "we were here first" and "if it weren't for me, you'd starve" and "why don't you just go back to the city?"

We farmers have shot ourselves in the proverbial foot by turning our neighbors into our enemies. And our neighbors would rather put us out of business than smell pesticides and chicken manure during their end-of-season soccer team chicken barbeque shindig.

The bottom line is this: a farm friendly food system is both aromatically and aesthetically pleasing. Anything else is not a good food system, period. End of discussion. If these criteria became the protocol for our food system, it would fundamentally change everything. And the changes would be for the better--especially for the plants and animals under our care.

God gave us senses for a reason. How do we tell if a wound is infected? By smell. How do we tell if a farm is infected? By smell. How do we tell if our child is feeling a little under the weather? Cheek color. How do we tell a vibrant rose? Color. Who wins the flower contest at the monthly garden club, the one with the most vibrant color or the member who brings the pale, drab-petalled flower?

Intuitively, we understand all of this and yet our culture continues to defend a food system that is neither pretty nor aromatically pleasing. One rule of thumb I use is this: Every single part of the food system should be such that a kindergarten class would enjoy sitting in its vicinity for an hour. Who wants to take their kindergarten class on a nature hike right after the herbicide application went through? Who wants to take their kindergarten class to enjoy communing with the hogs in a Smithfield pig factory?

As far as I'm concerned, the same is true beyond the farm, from packing, processing, slaughtering--whatever--all the way to the plate. This includes the gene splice cannons and the irradiation chambers. Let's all go sit down and watch Sesame Street by the food irradiation machine. Doesn't that sound fun? To listen to the industrial bought-off scientists, that's a safer place than the farm's compost pile. And yet, intuitively, we know such nonsense is just nonsense. Somehow we desperately want to believe the credentialed untruth, the credentialed spin. But we do so to our peril, and the peril of our food system.

One of the reasons this issue is critical is because urban flight is a megapolitical trend that is escalating in our culture. We spent a century depopulating the countryside to feed the urban centers which grew up around factories, and now in the information economy we will spend the next century depopulating the urban centers as satellite uplinks from home offices become normative. This new freedom to live anywhere is putting more pressure on smelly food systems while at the same time creating nearby customers for neighbor friendly farmers.

Finally people are realizing that the cheap chicken at the supermarket or fast food joint is coming from that noxious neighbor. Food buyers are beginning to connect the dots. "Oh, yeah, this chicken came from that obnoxious farm. Gross!" And as these connections finally snap together in the frontal lobe--"Hellooo!" --people are gaining a new appreciation for food that is produced in aesthetically and aromatically pleasing ways.

When people come and sit down in a true diversified, farm friendly vegetable garden, their spirits are soothed, their countenance radiates, and their emotions rest. The same is true in a field of grazing cows, a paddock of pastured chickens, or a savannah of pigaerating hogs. Everything about the farmscape should be soothing, enjoyable, and pleasant. Obviously, if the farmer happens to be building a pond or constructing a road, some mayhem may be apparent. That's fine. No gain without pain. But the pain must be focused and temporary, or instead of building muscle, you tear it down.

So what makes a neighbor friendly aromatically and aesthetically pleasing farm? Here are some ideas:

- Freedom to explore. Does the farmer let you go where you want? Does he declare certain areas off limits? A neighbor friendly farm gives visitors freedom. What does it look like? It doesn't have to be immaculate, but it should have a sense of order about it. Do animals appear to be where they belong? Is the garden neat and tidy? Are the fruit trees vibrant, or full of dead branches and generally unkempt? Are the animals happy? What about gulleys in fields and the color of the pond water?

- How does it smell? Sniff deeply. Do you smell honeysuckle blossoms or manure? Do you smell that antiseptic odor of pesticide and herbicide, or the deep, earthy smell of compost?

- What do you hear? Do you hear the constant roar of machinery, or the buzzing of honeybees pollinating blossoms? Can you hear the birds, the water trickling in the brook, and the grass swishing in the breeze?

- Is there a sense of wildness in the landscape? Some of the most important neighbors to a farm are the wild critters that inhabit hedge and marsh. These perform vital functions to maintain a balanced ecosystem that provides food choice for would-be predators or control for potential pathogens. The three great environments of open land, forest land, and riparian areas should

19

intersect over and over. Monospecies of plants or animals never offer the varied cornucopia that is normative on neighbor friendly farms.

- Who is doing the work? Does the operation look like a throwback to slavery, or does the work environment make you feel comfortable and peaceful? What is the demeanor of the staff? Are they upbeat, friendly, vibrant, or are they negative, downcast, and complainy?

- Would you like to live on this farm? Downwind? At ground zero, home base? All year long? No misgivings? This is a real test.

Farm friendly food is produced by farmers who offer a positive sensual experience. Only you, the buyer, can determine what that is. But I can guarantee you that if the average person visited the average farm in this country, the average person would buy an acre and produce all their own food. Neighbor friendly farms are not average. They are few and far between. By ferreting them out and patronizing them, food buyers can gradually change communities and landscapes to be the vibrant ecosystems they should be.

Chapter 4

Open

N othing to hide. That's the moniker of a farm friendly producer. The average farmer who grows chickens for Tyson has not a clue what is even in the feed the chickens are ingesting.

The industrial food system thrives on keeping the brains off farm. Even the agricultural colleges seldom recognize knowledge contributions from their constituency. The fount of knowledge must originate with the credentialed academic community; anything else is suspect--unless it comes from a multinational corporation lab. Then it's gospel.

I have said to our customers for decades: "If you think we're giving the chickens antibiotics at 2 a.m., come on out and see us then. If you think we're spreading chemical fertilizer at midnight, come on out and have a look." Of course, Teresa adds: "If you come out, don't wake us up."

`We have maintained an unconditional open door policy forever because it is the only way to have a food system that maintains farms. The less autonomy farmers have to make their own decisions, the fewer farms there will be. Industrial empire building is all about consolidation and amalgamation. The steady decline in the number of farms and the consistent concentration of agricultural production can only occur when decisions are being made off site. It's the old economies of scale thing.

Open

The result of this off-farm decision-making power is less access to information at the local level. "What kind of corn is that you're planting?" the food buyer asks.

"Oh, it's the latest from Pioneer."

"Is it genetically modified?"

"I don't know. All I know is what's on the label. Here, read it for yourself and you'll know as much as I do."

You look at the label: "Hybrid 2341. 120 Day. 95 Percent Germination." There you have it. That's all the information you need. The big guys dispense as little information as possible. The whole industrial mindset operates in a world of intrigue and mystery because its worldview is militaristic, fear-based, and scarcity-oriented.

Compare that to the knowledge a grower of heirloom apples can tell you about his crop. "Yeah, I planted that tree 5 years ago from a graft that came from my Grandpappy's favorite tree. It got buggy so we finally had to cut it down, but not until we preserved a few new trees. This apple should be used for about 20 percent of the blend to make the best cider you can find. It'll cook, but it might be a little stiff so I tend to add just a little water to make the applesauce better. I've never seen this tree split bark in the spring, but it does have a bit of scab. Those apples we just use in the cider. . . . "

As long as you stand there, he will tell you about this apple. He can tell you why he planted it where he did, what year, how he prunes it. He can tell you why it has a scar on the main limb 3 feet out from the trunk. The point is he knows this tree and its fruit. Compare that to a huge commercial orchard in China shipping apples to the U.S., pruning with a machine and planting genetically engineered stock from some global nursery. Which outfit is more open, more transparent?

In this day of information-based everything, transparency is the buzzword. We want transparent accounting, hiring practices, promotion practices, and health plans. Should we expect anything less of our farmers and the food system? Or should we just by faith bumble along assuming that the food industry will look out for our best interests? Anyone who thinks Wall Street is conscientiously looking out for your best interest and mine needs to have their head examined. They're out to

23

get theirs. And don't you forget it. That's not to say they are necessarily evil, it is just to say that the industrial business world seldom operates with a functional moral compass.

When you visit an open farm, you will not see no-trespassing signs (except maybe for bureaucrats) and door locks. The farmer will freely discuss his program with you. That program includes soil management, expenses, profit margins, successes and failures.

Few things irritate me more than to hear about supposedly organic or clean food producers who refuse to give out their chicken ration because it is a "trade secret." Too often, this phrase is used as a euphemistic justification for some sort of practice that customers would find offensive. Dodging openness under the guise of "proprietary information" is simply saying you're not good enough to preserve your constituency if someone else found out what you do. Good farming is an art as much as a science. Artists do not fear competition as much as technicians.

Personal character makes all the difference, not just the formula. The best chicken ration in the world won't make up for sloppy waterers, shoddy care, and dirty bedding. I've watched hundreds of farmers get "the formula" for some practice, touted as the magic bullet, the be all and end all, the thing that made Joe Schmoe a millionaire tycoon, only to fall flat on their face trying to duplicate it because they lacked an essential character quality like discipline, faithfulness, or attentiveness.

I've tried to start dozens of pastured poultry producers within 50 miles of us--and we live on a dirt road where the only time you have to lock your car is in August to keep the neighbors from putting runaway zucchini squash in it--only to have them give up after a year or two. Why? Lots of reasons. It can be anything from a divorce to being too meticulous to not wanting to care for the birds until after the second cup of coffee. Chickens wake up early.

Plenty of horticulturalists have shared their production secrets. Some folks take these tips and run with them, and others never get their enterprises off the ground. How many people stick with their New Years' Resolutions? How many people stick with anything? Their marriage? Their dreams?

Open

That is why I don't fear competition, and I've found that the best producers are the ones that share this view. The truth is that food buyers need to know the producers' world as much as the producer needs to know the buyers' world. Otherwise, each develops assumptions about the other and you have the distrusting situation we have in our food system today where most buyers believe farmers don't care about them, and farmers for sure believe buyers don't care about their welfare.

The result is that each side believes the other doesn't give a lick about their welfare. And continually putting a plethora of middlemen, teamsters, warehouses, and 1,500 miles between them doesn't help matters any. A farmer who buys into that system can't be very open because by and large most of his decisions are being made for him by the processor, packer, or whatever. He can be open about the fact that he doesn't know much, but that's about it.

How can you identify an open farm friendly food producer? Here are some tips:

- Communication. Does he return your phone calls, respond to your letters? Does he send a newsletter packed with real failure and success stories about the farm? Any spirit of secretiveness is a red flag. The operative term is communicate, communicate, communicate.

- Does he listen to you? Are the explanations for why he does or does not have a certain product you're interested in complete, plausible, and satisfying? Does he act too busy for your questions? Is he relaxed when you're asking questions, or does he seem ill at ease, furtive, and defensive?

- Are all doors and buildings accessible? How about the farmhouse? Do you feel like you can walk in and be welcome? Is the farmer up front and aggressive about encouraging you to go look at things and make yourself at home?

- Has the farmer ever told you that you cannot come at a certain time? I'm not talking here about being obnoxious. All of us food friendly farmers have our horror stories about the customer from hell. I have a couple of those who I'm sure would say I'm the most arrogant, closed, discourteous person they've ever met. But if that were normative, I wouldn't have a business. The point

25

here is what is off limits? We routinely let customers come to see the chickens processed--8-year-old boys enjoy taking the knife and slitting a throat. The parents are fainting and the kids are having a great time.

- Does the farmer have an unforced, ready rationale for variety selection, breeding, fertility program, feeding criteria, vaccination, and all the other practices you may find interesting? Sometimes the best answer is "we've always done it that way." But such an answer should always be the last resort and offered with openness: "But we're always ready to do it differently if there's a better way."

In the end, only you as a food buyer can determine if the openness satisfies your curiosity. But be willing to ask--even pester-- with questions to be assured that the farm decisions are being made there, that the knowledge base is emanating from the on-site staff rather than some boardroom in the next state. Openness from the producer is absolutely critical in the quest for farm friendly food.

Farm Friendly Product

Chapter 5

Soils and Fertility

F arm friendly food originates from fertile soils. The notion that farming wears out soils, or somehow depletes fertility, comes from many historical records, but is not necessarily true. Just because something happened does not mean it has to have happened.

While it is true that most civilizations have risen and fallen with the fertility of their soils, every culture had within its grasp the tools and techniques necessary to avert the disaster. Shortsightedness and mining the soil, while commonplace, are certainly avoidable. Choosing food producers who maintain their soils rather than depleting them is certainly necessary to a farm friendly food system. No farm can produce anything without productive soils.

The most fertile virgin soils in the world exist under prairie grasses and forests. Several observations come to mind when looking at these soils: They do not undergo tillage; a perennial plant covers the earth like a blanket. Mature leaves and plant material falls on top of the soil. Therefore the carbon falling to the earth is lignified rather than succulent vegetable material. It is not incorporated except by earthworms and other soil critters. Large animals are part and parcel of the ecosystem. Essentially nothing is brought in from outside the bioregion and nothing is exported from the bioregion. It is self maintaining. Flora and fauna are diversified and interdependent.

Soils and Fertility

Perhaps the greatest soil scientist of all time, Sir Albert Howard in his classic An Agricultural Testament, stated it as succinctly as anyone ever could:

> *"The main characteristic of Nature's farming can therefore be summed up in a few words. Mother earth never attempts to farm without livestock; she always raises mixed crops; great pains are taken to preserve the soil and to prevent erosion; the mixed vegetable and animal wastes are converted into humus; there is no waste; the processes of growth and the processes of decay balance one another; ample provision is made to maintain large reserves of fertility; the greatest care is taken to store the rainfall; both plants and animals are left to protect themselves against disease."*

While many organic producers and environmentalists today like to point to Justus von Liebig as the great Satan for establishing chemical fertilization because he did not value the role of humus, plenty of civilizations, for millennia, had destroyed their soils and their cultures for the same reason. Failure to maintain an active decomposition cycle through the decay and humus building process depletes soils of their nutrients, resiliency, and water retentive capacity.

Any good landscaper will mulch flower beds and around trees with some sort of decomposable, carbonaceous material. When you lift this mulch with a garden trowel, you see a veritable village of critters living underneath it. This is the life in the soil. Acidulated chemical fertilizers which burn the little cut on your hand also burn these inhabitants in the soil. A living soil contains as many critters in a double handful as there are people on the face of the earth. It is not just some inert material holding up plants. It is the stomach of the earth, the nurturer of all sustenance.

The link between healthy soils and healthy plants and animals is so well established I will not bore you with an apologetic connecting the two. The point I want to make here is that, amazingly, much of the food grown in America does not come from fertile soil. It is nutritionally depleted. And just because soils grow volumes of stuff does not mean they are fertile.

Holy Cows and Hog Heaven

Growth is not inherently better any more than turning up the volume makes bad music better. Just because a farm is filling bins and bushels with food does not mean the food is fit to eat. Remember, cancer is a growth--unregulated and uncontrolled growth. Does anyone want to see a growth in the number of wars? The number of abortions? The number of high school dropouts?

And yet we worship growth as if it is the noblest goal in the world. Does anyone think it healthy to add 50 lbs.? Of course not, unless you suffer from bulimia. Through modern technology, we have learned to produce bins and bushels without nutrient content. It's like giving tons of high school diplomas without knowing the information.

All of us are familiar with supermarket cardboard tomatoes and tasteless apples. The industrial food system does not care a lick about nutrition. The goals are volume and handling ability--enough toughness to take mechanical harvest, boxing and jostling around in a tractor trailer for 1,500 miles, then sit on a supermarket shelf for a week without decomposing.

One sign of a nutritionally superior apple is the rapidity with which it turns brown when you bite into it. A really good apple browns before you can even eat the skin off all the way around. In fact, current research indicates that it is that browning that correlates with the anti-carcinogenic qualities of the fruit. It relates to antioxidants and all that jazz.

I am neither a soil scientist nor a food nutritionist, but I promise that the mainline American food system mocks both soil life and nutrition. Obesity is pandemic. There is a reason why grocery stores have all teamed up with pharmacies. When the depleted food doesn't make people healthy, they have to prop themselves up with drugs.

Again I turn to Howard:

"Artificial manures lead inevitably to artificial nutrition, artificial food, artificial animals, and finally to artificial men and women. The ease with which crops can be grown with chemicals has made the correct utilization of wastes much more difficult. If a cheap substitute for humus exists, why not use it? The answer is twofold.

Soils and Fertility

In the first place, chemicals can never be a substitute for humus because Nature has ordained that the soil must live and the mycorrhizal association must be an essential link in plant nutrition. In the second place, the use of such a substitute cannot be cheap because soil fertility-- one of the most important assets of any country--is lost; because artificial plants, artificial animals, and artificial men are unhealthy and can only be protected from the parasites, whose duty it is to remove them, by means of poison sprays, vaccines and serums and an expensive system of patent medicines, panel doctors, hospitals, and so forth. When the finance of crop production is considered together with that of the various social services which are needed to repair the consequences of an unsound agriculture, and when it is borne in mind that our greatest possession is a healthy, virile population, the cheapness of artificial manures disappears altogether. In the years to come chemical manures will be considered as one of the greatest follies of the industrial epoch."

How about that for a 1943 Oxford University publication? It's been way more than half a century since Howard penned those eloquent lines, and here we are feeding poultry manure to cows, burning cow manure in electric generation plants, and powering prison boilers with sawdust. Shame on us, shame on us, shame on us. Such abuse of nature's bounty is unconscionable, and conventional supermarket fare along with non-thinking, disconnected food buying, promotes such an immoral system.

How do you know if your food is grown on fertile soil, if it is the real thing? Here is a checklist for the food buyer:

- Ask the farmer about his fertility program. Listen for words like "organic matter," "cover crops", "green manures", and "trace minerals." Red flags include: "plant food," "urea," "NPK," and "recommended fertilizer applications."

- Ask to see the compost pile. Compost is the lifeblood of any natural fertility program, especially a viable farm friendly commercial operation. Compost piles are litmus tests for genuine clean food producers.

31

- Check the soil in the garden or under the fruit. Is it black, loamy, and full of soil life, including earthworms? Is it covered or open? The soil should be loose and friable, not hard or packed. It should crumble in your hand, not containing hard balls. It should have a rich, earthy odor, not sterile or antiseptic.

- Are grapevines, orchard trees, strawberries and other fruits or perennial nut bearing plants mulched or is the soil tilled up around the base and the soil laid bare? This technique encourages earlier fruiting due to radiant heat, but it destroys soil.

- Ask to see the carbon inventory, especially if it is a livestock farm. Any commercial honest food farm will store piles of old hay, sawdust, wood chips, straw, corn fodder, leaves or other carbon-rich materials so that no manure is handled or spread raw. Liquid manure systems are a no-no. The whole point is to keep manure out of the water, not put it in the water. If this is a cattle ranch in a brittle (low-rainfall) environment, its carbon storage is on the forage inventoried in the field ahead of the cows. Carbon should be inventoried in some form somewhere.

- Walk the fields and look for earthworm castings. These slightly gummy mounds can be anywhere from a quarter inch to an inch tall. A healthy soil should boast half a dozen per square foot. If you have to look far, it's not good soil. Drought will drop the earthworm activity.

- Taste leafy vegetables. Are they sweet or bitter? Organic matter buffers the soil. Cabbage, lettuce, and Swiss chard should be pleasantly mild or even sweet with high sugar content. Cucumbers and carrots should be sweet to the taste. Sugars can be measured with a refractometer, which measures a brix reading of the juice.

- Is there any bare ground around animal facilities? That's a no-no. Animals should be on clean bedding or lush green vegetation. No dirt chicken yards.

Chapter 6

Food is Biological

F ood is fundamentally a biological process. While industry has enabled us to substitute machinery for much hand labor, it can never create food. Honest nutritionists hold to the general rule that real food rots. If it won't rot, it's not real food.

That is not a bad yardstick for the hurried and harried food buyer. How can you tell if it's real food? Set it on the counter for a couple of days. If it grows mold and begins to decompose, it's probably alive and can feed your body. If it doesn't, it's probably industrial pseudo food that isn't worth a dime or may even be unhealthy.

Just so we're on the same page, let's think about some things that won't rot on the kitchen counter:

- Hershey's kisses. You can leave the leftovers from last Christmas on the counter until doom's day, and they'll still be right like you left them. Sweet and ready to eat.

- Granola bars. You can take them on a trip or camping in the woods, save the leftovers until next year, and they'll taste and look just like they did fresh out of the store.

- Breakfast cereal. Indestructible.

Food is Biological

Most unprocessed foods require refrigeration or freezing. The most obvious exception to this rule is nuts. But even they will go stale over time once they are cracked out of their shell. Vegetables and fruits, left on the counter, will deteriorate within a couple of days. Industrial apples will hold up for a long time. Heirloom varieties won't.

That brings us to this idea of biology. Food should be living. Really living. Something happens once the industrial processing corporations get their hands on it that fundamentally changes the food. Compare the rotting speed of raw potatoes to potato chips. Compare the rotting speed of fresh whole wheat bread to how long you can leave white enriched bread on the table.

Living food cannot always be sensed with the naked eye. But animals can tell. I had a customer whose husband razzed her about coming out to a farm to buy ground beef. He said it was all the same and she might as well get the cheap stuff where she bought everything else anyway. The one stop shop deal. She had this pet cat who would always come running when it smelled fresh meat, but it would never eat any. For years this cat refused to eat any ground beef when this lady would drop it a morsel or two.

When she returned home with our meat that evening and opened the package to fix supper, here came the cat. In normal loving tones, she scolded the feline: "What are you coming around here for? You never like this stuff anyway. Get out of here." But the cat stayed and rubbed and pushed and looked up pleadingly until finally the lady relented and dropped a pinch of meat. The cat lunged on it and devoured it.

Right at that instant, the lady's husband walked into the kitchen and saw the cat. He said to his wife: "I don't know where you got that meat, but from now on, that's all I'm going to eat." She related this story to me and I could hardly believe it. The next week we did a food fair exhibit and cooked a pound of our ground beef and a pound of ground round--the good stuff--that we purchased at the supermarket.

The four quarter pound paddies that we made sat out in the sun all day so we didn't want to eat them when we got home. Having four cats, we decided to take advantage of the situation and see if we could replicate the customer's experience. We put the paddies on two separate plates and set them down for the four cats. The cats sniffed both, then immediately licked up all four of ours and almost consumed the paper plate before they would even lick the supermarket meat on the other plate. We took pictures of it. The lesson here? When in doubt about your food, ask your pet.

Pets aren't swayed by peer pressure. They aren't bought off by big business fat cats (no pun intended). They are just adorable, honest assessors, and they will render a true opinion. This story widens the definition of junk food. As one of our customers testified in a General Assembly hearing: "I've found that 90 percent of the food in the grocery story is injurious to my health."

Perhaps no one captures the spirit of the industrial food system better than Eric Schlosser in his highly acclaimed book <u>Fast Food Nation</u>. In one section he tells about his visit to the New Jersey flavor industry.

> *"A number of companies sell sophisticated devices that attempt to measure mouthfeel. The Universal TA-XT2 Texture Analyzer, produced by the Texture Technologies Corporation, performs calculations based on data derived from twenty-five separate probes. It is essentially a mechanical mouth. It gauges the most important rheological properties of a food--the bounce, creep, breaking point, density, crunchiness, chewiness, gumminess, lumpiness, rubberiness, springiness, slipperiness, smoothness, softness, wetness, juiciness, spreadability, springback, and tackiness."*

Doesn't it make your mouth water? Is anybody asking the 3 trillion microbes that inhabit each person's intestines what they would like? Doesn't it make sense to ask them? We live in such a paranoid age that I'm convinced if you walked down the sidewalk in Anytown, USA and asked any soccer mom if she knew she had 3 trillion bacteria inhabiting her insides, she would convulse into a heap of spasmodic ranting: "Quick, cut me open and pour in the Lysol!"

In a day of unprecedented interest in nature, hiking, camping, aquariums and nature-type videos, we've failed to consider the interconnectedness of our outside world and our inside digestion and assimilation process. What feeds these bacteria is not Archer Daniels Midland amalgamated, reconstituted, chlorinated, extruded, extracted,

Food is Biological

adulterated, irradiated, genetically prostituted, inhumane, globally transported, disrespected protoplasmic pseudo food. These bacteria don't know anything about Wall Street, the religious right or the liberal left. But if we don't care what they want, we disrespect the very foundation of life.

The laws of physics occur in the biological world just as surely as they do in the mechanical. For every action there is an equal but opposite reaction. Food designed for extended shelf life will automatically suffer in taste and nutrition. The best food can ever be is when it is fresh. Storage takes a toll on every food item.

This is why animals on biologically sensitive farms are moved around from pasture to pasture onto fresh green salad bars. The freshness stimulates the ingestion of the green material. Fresh grass, for example, contains natural antibiotics that vaporize during the wilting process. Sure, cows can do okay on hay, but real thriving and production require fresh, vegetative forage.

Blackberries picked off the vine and consumed on the spot are always more tasty and nutritious than they are after they've been refrigerated, frozen, put in pies, or canned into jams. Food life begins to deteriorate from the moment of harvest until consumption. That is why a food buyer connected to a real farm producing real food has the highest chance of eating on the highest nutritional plane.

John Ikerd, retired professor from the University of Missouri and an outspoken critic of industrial agriculture, says that the four pillars of industrial paradigms are:

1. Specialization
2. Simplification
3. Routinization
4. Mechanization

In contrast, biological pillars are:

1. Diversification
2. Complexity
3. Flexibility
4. Living

Holy Cows and Hog Heaven

Let's briefly examine these with respect to the food system and farms in particular.

SPECIALIZED VS. DIVERSIFIED   Industrial farms and farmers view themselves as monospecies producers. Apple growers, vegetable producers, cattlemen--these are the titles of most farmers. And their farms illustrate the point: corn and soybeans; poultry; vineyard.

A biological system, however, is highly multispeciated. A farm that mimics nature and therefore has a better chance of surviving over the long haul will produce a variety of plants and animals and even variety within those varieties. A biological food system is like a horn of plenty, sporting a multitude of cascading variety.

Healthy landscapes are not monocultures; they are polycultures. Many if not most of the problems afflicting agriculture are symptoms of monospeciation. Chickens sanitize pastures behind grazing herbivores; sheep graze orchards; pigs eat dairy and especially cheese residues; chickens debug orchards and vineyards; thin-canopied nut trees provide a second tier of solar collection above vineyards.   These are all relationships that a biological farmer appreciates and incorporates into production models.

SIMPLIFIED VS. COMPLEX   Industrial farmers follow formulas while biological farmers follow observations. The difference is huge. Many farmers who grow chickens for the vertically integrated industry know how to solve their production problems, but the company field representatives will not approve the changes. The chicken is just a pile of protoplasmic matter.

Even the most simplified landscapes are a complex network of plants, animals, bacteria, minerals and water. Compare the complexity of native prairie, with each acre growing approximately 40 species of perennial grasses, forbes, weeds, and herbs, to the same plowed acre growing only corn or soybeans.

Consider this difference by extension to the herbivore, which was created with four stomachs to convert this perennial prairie and all its species into meat and milk. Now consider this same wonderfully complex animal being fed a diet of 100 percent corn or corn silage from the monocropped corn field. And then we wonder why this beef doesn't contain the B vitamins, the conjugated linoleic acid, the polyunsaturated

38

Food is Biological

fatty acids, of its perennial polyculture grazing counterpart?

Compare a carrot grown in 10-10-10 chemical fertilizer every year compared to one grown in compost-fertilized soil covered in mulch. When farmers were told that all they needed was nitrogen, potassium, and phosphorus, it did a great disservice to everyone who eats food.

ROUTINE VS. FLEXIBLE Consistency in the front door and out the back door is critical for the smooth running factory. But potatoes don't all look the same. Seasons are different--some wet and some dry. Nature is flexible, or dynamic. It changes every day. Floods, droughts, hurricanes, epidemics--the face of nature is ever fresh, ever new. Birth, youth, maturity and finally death is in direct contradiction to the routine. Nature is full of variables, full of changes.

Few aspects of American agriculture illustrate this better than Confinement Animal Feeding Operations (CAFOs). These monstrous buildings have the same animals in them all year round, year after year after year. No rest. No change. Just a consistent buildup of pathogencity and a blind trust in the cleverness of scientists to concoct more powerful brews from the Devil's pantry to knock down the bad bugs.

The same is true for large scale vegetable and crop production. Attend any crop symposium today and 90 percent of the discussion will be about disease. Part of the problem is concentration like plant spacing, but most of it is due to lack of variability. A century ago before chemicals were widely used even vegetables were rotated between years of pasture and small grain. Today, methyl bromide fumigates the soil so that strawberries can be grown on the same ground year after year after year. No change.

MECHANIZED VS. LIVING A machine responds the same way every time you push a lever. But living things have a mind of their own.

The same cuddly expressions to your wife that elicit romantic results one night can elicit sighs and consternation the next. Living things move, breathe, and fascinate us with mystery.

We can take apart a plant to its cells, to its molecules, and even to its electrons, protons and neutrons, but we cannot put it back together

39

again. There is a mystery of life that far exceeds the human grasp, and a reverential distance that must be maintained when dealing with life. In our mechanistic view we arrogate divinity to ourselves, and say: "I think the pig should have been made this way."

Life is not inert. How dare we approach life as if it were just as subject to our discretion as a lump of clay, an iron ingot, a spinning mass of plastic fiber? The result of mechanical food is mechanical people--lifeless, bored, depressed and void of meaning.

Here are some tips in your quest for biological food:

- Make sure it comes from a biologically-based farm. A farm that exhibits these principles will have the tell-tale signs as indicated in the checklist for soil fertility at the end of the previous chapter.

- Who packed and processed the food? The bigger the entity, the more likely it has been devitalized for the sake of shelf life, stability, and handling qualities.

- Eat as close to the source as possible. Get it at the farmgate. Join a Community Supported Agriculture (CSA) farm. Buy at the farmers' market. Farmers who sell directly to consumers are not philosophically pressured to produce cardboard tomatoes and juiceless apples.

- The less processing, the better. Precooking, preseasoning, preparing all take a toll. Maintaining product taste and appearance stability almost always requires manipulation that is foreign to your 3 trillion intestinal critters.

Chapter 7

East vs. West

The United States is a culture predicated on a decidedly western interpretation of the world. This view is rooted in the systematic reasoning and deductive logic of Greco-Roman thought. It permeated Europe and migrated with the colonists to the New World.

At the risk of being overly simplistic, this worldview essentially looks at pieces as the key to the whole. Its key words are compartmentalized, disconnected, fragmented, reductionist, linear, and it glorifies the individual. It gave us systematic theology and Deism. It studies parts rather than wholes.

This view gave us Crusaders and Conquistadors. It also gave us the Renaissance, front end loaders, electric lights and the Age of Discovery. It gave us electric fences, plastic wrap, and manure spreaders. Hurray for western thought!

But wait just a minute. An equally valid worldview comes from the east. It studies the whole rather than the parts. Key words are interrelated, holism, community, we instead of I. It tends to give human characteristics to the natural world, like Mother Earth.

This view has given us Judaism, Hinduism, and eastern religion. It spawned deep ecology, the environmental movement and a reverence for nature. The clean food movement, wellness centers, and Yoga sprang out of eastern thought. Native Americans were eastern. White

42

East vs. West

Anglo Saxon Protestants were western.

Taking the best of both worlds provides balance. Unfortunately, appreciating both is practically impossible. Neither one easily coexists with the other. Eastern thinkers worshipping and reverencing lightning never considered that it could be harnessed as electricity. Native Americans rather enjoyed being able to hunt buffalo with western .30-.30 caliber lever action Winchester rifles, but they still reverenced the animals and did not seek to annihilate them. The same rifles in the hands of western Conquistadors, however, resulted in the annihilation of the buffalo.

Eastern thought provides the moral boundary around the cleverness of western discovery. This worldview and cultural clash is nothing new. One of my favorite historical passages comes from June 17, 1744, when the commissioners from Maryland and Virginia negotiated a treaty with the Indians of the Six Nations at Lancaster, Pennsylvania in which the Indians were invited to send boys to William and Mary College. Here is the response from the Indians:

"We know that you highly esteem the kind of learning taught in those Colleges, and that the Maintenance of our young Men, while with you, would be very expensive to you. We are convinced, that you mean to do us Good by your Proposal; and we thank you heartily. But you, who are wise must know that different Nations have different Conceptions of things and you will therefore not take it amiss, if our Ideas of this kind of Education happen not to be the same as yours. We have had some Experience of it. Several of our young People were formerly brought up at the Colleges of the Northern Provinces: they were instructed in all your Sciences; but, when they came back to us, they were bad runners, ignorant of every means of living in the woods . . . neither fit for Hunters, Warriors, nor Counselors, they were totally good for nothing.

We are, however, not the less oblig'd by your kind Offer, tho' we decline accepting it; and, to show our grateful Sense of it, if the Gentlemen of Virginia will send us a Dozen of their Sons, we will take Care of their Education, instruct them in all we know, and make Men of them."

Holy Cows and Hog Heaven

Wouldn't it have been neat if the westerners had appreciated this offer instead of dismissing it as worthless knowledge from a bunch of pagan barbarians who didn't even have enough sense to powder their wigs and build cobblestone streets? What a shame that we could not have coexisted and learned from each other. The Indians could have enjoyed some labor saving machinery and the Colonists could have learned about native medicinal plants and living lightly on the land.

Unfortunately, just like what usually happens when eastern and western worldviews come into contact, one had to dominate and conquer the other. As I write this on a decidedly western contrivance, a MacIntosh computer, my heart aches for the earthworms destroyed by chemical fertilizers. This is the kind of dual appreciation that can move us forward.

What typically happens, though, is that the environmentalist moves toward an imbalanced hatred of everything western and the westerner labels everything eastern as so much metaphysical hocus pocus. Just as I'd like to ask Don Tyson how many chicken houses are enough, I'd like to ask the Nature Conservancy how many wilderness areas are enough. The western ranchers using the property rights mantra to justify overgrazing and desertification are just as wrong as the Buffalo Commons folks who view private ownership of property as one of the seven deadly sins.

This struggle is certainly apparent in the clean food arena. One of the biggest dilemmas facing the organic food movement right now is how to take a decidedly eastern connected holistic product and sell it through a decidedly western disconnected Wall Streetified marketing scheme. Now that the government has assumed ownership of the movement by defining the word "organic," the modern bluecoat Seventh Cavalry bureaucrats are slowly and methodically doing their double duty:

1. Wipe out the nonconformists by either exterminating them or putting them on a reservation where they can be controlled.

2. Entice the rest to sign away their autonomy and their culture through treaties that will inevitably homogenize the differences and gradually nullify any impact from an alternative view.

East vs. West

True progress comes when we marry eastern indigenous heritage wisdom with appropriate western techno-glitzy discoveries to create synergism and symbiosis. A good example of this is the new electrified poultry netting. It is polyethylene webbing with stainless steel threads woven through it. The plastic provides strength; the metal provides conductivity for an electric current. By using highly technical low impedance energizers that can shorten the electric pulse to microseconds, a high voltage shock can be delivered through the threads without melting the plastic.

This fence is now used all over the world by farm friendly poultry producers to keep black bears, coyotes, dogs, raccoons and skunks out of the chickens while keeping the chickens in. The fence can be moved easily every couple of days to give the poultry a fresh pasture paddock. It can be meandered through an orchard or vineyard as well. Who would have thought 50 years ago that you could have a fence that could keep bears and coyotes out, and chickens and turkeys in, that would weigh only 12 pounds per 150 feet and could be put up or taken down in 10 minutes? When dovetailed with lightweight portable hoophouse structures mounted on skids, these systems allow a modern farmer to raise chickens in a more chicken friendly environment, more hygienically, with better sanitation and predator protection, producing a more nutritious product, than a backyard flock on an American homestead. Wow!

Farm friendly food asks the question: "Is the pig happy?" On our farm and thousands like it, we try to provide a habitat to each plant and animal that allows it to fully express its physiological distinctiveness. When we respect nature or the Creator's design enough to reverence the plow on the end of a pig's nose, the graceful beak on the front of a chicken, the earthworms gamboling around in the soil underneath the cabbages, then we have a moral framework in which to contain our human cleverness.

Honest food uses nature as a template, placed over the production model, to duplicate domestically what nature does in the wild. Our responsibility as stewards is to enhance these principles, not override them. In nature, for example, herbivores never eat grain, fermented forage, or carrion. I don't need a scientist to tell me feeding chicken manure and grain to cows is not a good thing to do. My eastern framework dictates that I not feed cows those things even if I can, and even if it makes them grow faster, and even if they seem to like it.

Do you feed your children candy bars just because they like them? How many of us like things that aren't good for us? If you put enough sugar on it, I could probably eat cow manure. That's why the industry puts molasses in urea lick tanks and mixes in molasses and corn silage with chicken manure--to make it palatable for the cows.

In the movie Jurassic Park, the professor is euphoric over the success of his program to resurrect long extinct dinosaurs. The dinosaurs are eating cars with people in them, tearing down the park fences and obviously getting ready to destroy civilization. While the scientist celebrates, the journalist has the audacity to ask him: "But just because we can, should we?"

That is a pregnant question, and one we would do well to ask ourselves every day. Just because we can feed corn to cows, should we? Just because we can plow up a 25 acre field and plant it in strawberries, should we? Just because we can airfreight certified organic cut flowers from Lima, Peru to San Francisco overnight, should we? Just because we can ship certified organic yogurt from a Vermont dairy to Sacramento, should we? Just because we can buy San Joaquin Valley certified organic tomatoes in New York City in February, should we?

Fast growth, profit margins, and efficiencies--these are only noble goals as long as the bigger reference for life is maintained.

Happy pigs and happy cabbages provide the most nutritious food and require the least amount of pharmaceutical intervention. As an extension of this idea, I would even suggest that our ability to coexist with people who are a little different than us is directly related to how we respect the differences in the plants and animals.

The ultimate disconnect--what in debate we used to call intellectual schizophrenia--is for patrons of environmental organizations to take their grandchildren or children by McDonald's for Happy Meals. I'm not suggesting that it is necessarily sin to ever darken the door of a fast food establishment, but once a week is ridiculous--if we care. And many people are in one daily.

The western industrial paradigm raised a generation of infants on Enfamil and Similac because the eastern natural art of breastfeeding was considered barbaric in the 1950s. This resulted in thousands of allergy sufferers and asthmatics. As the pendulum corrected itself through the hippie movement and Woodstock, the beaded, bearded, braless revolution created La Leche League, massage centers, and a new respect for alternative medicine and herbal remedies.

This whole shift is a correction to the cultural pendulum that swung too far toward the industrial model. Religiously, the charismatic movement was an eastern answer to stodgy western catechisms. The truth is that each side can benefit from respecting the assets that the other brings to the table.

The non-industrial food movement is a direct response to over-industrialization, the disrespectful mechanistic view toward everything living. This search for meaning, for the soul of food, is driving everything alternative. These are interesting times for our western culture. Watching the disequilibria that occurs as these two worldviews jockey for position is both thrilling and terrifying.

Historically, eastern views have not fared well when confronted with westerners. Consider the Native Americans. Consider the Incas. Consider the Aztecs. Wall Street and the western bureaucracy will not take erosion of its market share kindly. Farm friendly producers and farm friendly food buyers need to be vigilant about the cultural clash. Knowing about it is empowering.

So what does an eastern food system look like? Miles of monocrops, Archer Daniels Midland, and Wal-Mart represent the quintessential soulless western food system. Here are some characteristics of a more eastern one.

- Nonhybrid species, open pollinated, heritage breeds, or farm specific genetics. Any or all of these may play a part, but the idea is a respect for genetic diversity, including enjoying recessive trait surprises.

- Food with a face. Michael Olson, author of MetroFarm likes this phrase to describe the relationship that a food buyer can cultivate with the producer. To know that when you sit down and eat your applesauce, you can describe the orchard where they were grown. This adds a host of spiritual, emotional nuances to the food that far exceeds the simplistic western reductionist food pyramid.

- Indigenous foods and recipes. What Sally Fallon explains in her wonderful book <u>Nourishing Traditions</u> and Jo Robinson extols in her website *www.eatwild.com*. The idea is to eat like our ancestors ate to avoid the western degenerative diseases so rampant in our culture.

- Avoiding foods with unpronounceable ingredients or long ingredient lists. You can be sure than anything you can't read is probably disconnected from your 3 trillion intestinal critters.

- Few or no bells, beepers and bar codes. Rather, look for handwritten invoices, hugs, and heartfelt conversation at the purchasing venue.

Chapter 8

Genetic Engineering

B ecause it is such a critical issue right now, let's spend just a bit focusing on genetic engineering. Farm friendly food is not genetically engineered.

Nothing in our society right now better represents the entrapment, enslavement, and elimination of farmers more dramatically than genetically engineered food. The biggest hoax in the world is that it is a product of science. That anyone who opposes genetic engineering is a Luddite and anti-science, anti-progress, anti-human because without it half the world will starve to death.

I was sitting at a conference table with a scientist the other day and he got in my face, demanding why I wanted to blind 500,000 oriental children. Genetically modified golden rice with vitamin A, he said, was the "only" solution for those children. He was incredulous that I could be so hard hearted as to want them all to be blind.

This is the kind of arrogance the conventional scientific community uses to bludgeon critics into submission. I have four responses to this scientist:

1. Practically nothing has only one solution. Anyone who would be so myopic as to suggest this oriental blindness is a one-solution problem exhibits the worst kind of provincialism. Even if I didn't have a better solution at the moment, such a statement is pedantic in the

extreme.

2. A child would have to eat 7 pounds of rice a day in order to ingest enough of the gene-spliced vitamin to do any good. Have you tried eating 7 pounds of rice recently?

3. A few ounces of the indigenous green herbaceous plants that used to grow around these paddies before herbicides were used will provide more than enough vitamins to eliminate the blindness. If these farms would let their native plants grow, they would not need the multinational corporate cure at all. All available for sale at a price, of course.

4.   The rice-only diet is a relative newcomer to the oriental culture anyway. The heritage diet included a huge variety of fish and meat and vegetables. The increase in per capita rice consumption does not show a rise in health, but a degradation of indigenous nutrition due to the influx of foreign experts and their government-subsidized infrastructure.

Remember the laws of physics--the equal and opposite reaction thing. Cell phones have ramped communication up to an extreme level, but how many people would like to rip that umbilical off and throw it into the ocean? Cars have become extremely quiet and sophisticated, but who can work on them anymore?

The point is that every technological solution has a down side, and we have to weigh benefits against risks. On our farm, for example, we use tractors and front end loaders to move mountains of compost. We recognize that there is a cost in petroleum and resources to build and maintain the tractor, but because of the additional carbon we're able to sequester through large-scale compost fertilization, we believe the benefits outweigh the risks. Horse farmers routinely take me to task for not farming with horses. I've always said the day I see a horse with a front end loader and PTO shaft, I'll buy one.

None of us is completely consistent. While this book deals with the optimum, all of us live in the real world of compromises. Of course you're going to be traveling sometime and stop at a burger joint. Of course a Super Bowl party requires pizza and Coke. But exceptions are not habits. And if the ideas espoused in this book became habits while the mainline habits of our culture became exceptions, it would fundamentally change our world.

So let's tackle genetic engineering, realizing that few things are totally good or totally bad. We operate in the world of marginal reactions and weak links. And it's in that context that we make decisions, not the all good or all bad context.

At the risk of being declared a raving lunatic, let me make a heretical declaration to set the stage for our discussion: Science is not objective.

Every day you can open the newspaper and see scientists warning about global warming. But the next day, a group of scientists says there's nothing to it, that actually we're heading for another ice age (a view I personally tend to think has more credence than the warming idea). One group of education scientists says teaching is best done one way and another group says their studies show it's another way.

Scientists promoted the high carbohydrate diet and now the popularity of Dr. Atkins is making them all run the other way. I saw this firsthand a couple of decades ago when land grant universities first began studying organic farming, using grant money from multinational corporations, of course.

They would take research plots that had been used to test herbicides, chemical fertilizer concoctions, or whatever, for years, and designate a couple of them as the "organic" plots. Adjacent would be the pair of conventional plots. They would plant corn in each pair. The conventional corn (always a hybrid of course) was duly sprayed and fertilized. The organic didn't receive anything. At the end of the season, they measured the production.

Of course, the "organic" corn produced pitifully and the conventional corn yielded multitudes of grain. Dutiful students measured the differences, plugged the numbers into the computer, and then wrote thesis papers showing that if organic farming were adopted worldwide, half the world would starve. Or, in the words of Dennis Avery, darling of everything farm unfriendly, we would plow down the world's rainforests and destroy half the planet's species to produce enough food to feed everyone.

Now folks, this credentialed, accredited, scientific experiment was as integrity-challenged as an abortionist who grabs a wiggling baby and calls it tissue. Anyone who knows anything about organic farming knows that it takes at least three years, and often more, to heal a chemicalized soil. It takes time for the soil culture, the soil life, to regain a virile foothold and begin doing all the highly productive things that these critters do.

Countless replicated, accredited studies in recent years have totally debunked those earlier skewed comparisons. But I remember well when our state's commissioner of agriculture said organic farming was like playing Russian roulette with the citizens; somebody just had to decide which half would die.

As a food buyer, you need to be steadfast in this truth that science is subjective. Otherwise you will be blown about every day with some new scientific finding. This is one reason you do not see a lot of science in this book. I am not opposed to science, but ultimately what we believe in our hearts trumps the facts. Our hearts screen out what does not fit our paradigm. I love to ask for a show of hands when I speak at sustainable agriculture conferences for how many have ever argued a neighbor into organic farming. Nobody ever has. Because you don't argue someone into something they refuse to see.

The old saying "I'll believe it when I see it" would be more accurately rendered "I'll see it when I believe it." We sent our pastured broilers to an accredited food sciences lab to get a fat profile analysis. We also sent a regular fecal supermarket brand. The professor didn't want to do the test because he said there would be no difference, that chicken was chicken. Just look at the generic USDA label--there's a nutrition label for every commodity.

We persevered and he finally did the test. The fats were so different the computer had trouble graphing them on one sheet of paper. It almost required little squiggly infinity lines. When the professor handed the test to us, he said: "See, I told you there wouldn't be any difference." If he admitted that a difference existed, he would become responsible for that new information. His life would no longer be business as usual. The expedient thing to do was bury his head in the sand and not see anything. Then he could go along his jolly tenured way and continue being backslapped and loved by his multinational patron saints. This is the real world of our institutions of higher learning.

Holy Cows and Hog Heaven

In his fabulous book <u>Seeds of Deception</u> Jeff Smith names people, places, and studies that were purposely adulterated by blue chip multinational corporations to present genetic engineering in a positive light. I'll share one technique just so you'll get a flavor for what he presents.

Feeding trials on rats vary greatly depending on what kind of animal you use and what you measure at the end. One favorite gimmick used by industry researchers when putting together their dossier for the government agencies that approve or disapprove the product is to use mature rats rather than young ones. When an animal's physiology is mature, it is not nearly as susceptible to food abnormalities.

This is why children are much more susceptible to environmental toxins than adults. Their tissues are growing faster and therefore are more affected by dietary or pathogenic nuances.

In genetic feeding trails, the industries use mature rats. And then they do not even weigh the organs at the end of the study. In Scotland, where the research was duplicated using young rats and measuring organs, dramatic affects of the genetically engineered food was documented. Brains were smaller, livers were smaller, growth was retarded, behavior affected. Tremendous negative consequences.

So when the scientists say: "This food is safe because we've tested it" it is an entirely subjective statement. You can go to the bank with it with as much confidence as if your three year old comes to you with a genuine personally-created Crayola three dollar bill. It's that credible.

As a culture we have to get over this infatuation with science as if it speaks Ex Cathedra every Monday morning in USA TODAY. The science is only as good as the integrity of the patrons. And when we're talking about global market share and billions of dollars, lots of integrity can get compromised.

Now for some specific arguments against genetic engineering.

1. It violates God's Genesis plan: "And God said, 'Let the earth bring forth grass, the herb yielding seed, and the fruit tree yielding fruit after his kind, whose seed is in itself, upon the earth: ' and it was so." Gen. 1:11. This command gives two imperatives:

Genetic Engineering

    A. The plants should reproduce from their own seed.

    B. The seed should germinate true--children should look like parents.

This imperative is totally abrogated by genetic engineering. In the first place, the seeds are patented and sterility is engineered in so that plants cannot reproduce. This is why pollen drift is such a big problem. If your genetically engineered pollen drifts over my multi-generationally seed-saved field, it can wipe out generations of breeding and cultivar development.

Secondly, the seed that does germinate does not reproduce true to kind. Even the plants are not true to kind. Now we have a tomato that's part pepper and part pork. So when a devout Jew or Moslem or vegetarian goes to the store to buy tomatoes, she is eating parts of pork. It's really loused up.

Anyone who has a shred of belief in a Creator's design should dismiss genetic engineering outright. That alone is enough to discredit it.

    2. It is totally unnecessary to feed the world. The world is awash in food. Half the food imported to India every year gets eaten by sacred rats. That is not a food problem; that is a social/religious/cultural problem. No one starves in the world because there is not enough food. People starve because western foreign aid goes in with promises of better seeds and the people throw away their time-proven indigenous crop varieties. These new varieties demand inputs the people can't afford.

Or they starve because some local chieftain won't let the Red Cross truck cross land under his control. The whole food shortage cry is a myth. And to justify any technology with the risks inherent in genetic engineering on the basis of this despicable food shortage myth is a crime against creation and humanity equivalent to the Holocaust.

If you get a copy of the old USDA <u>Yearbooks of Agriculture</u> when the Green Revolution was just gearing up, you will see the identical phraseology used to justify DDT, chemical fertilizers and the whole organophosphate family. The phrases used to justify genetic engineering have been lifted, verbatim, right out of those old apologetics.

The truth is that obese people are starving to death for real nutrition. And we don't need genetic engineering to offer the world real nutrition.

3. It will create safer food. The only reason we have unsafe food in our country is because of the amalgamated, centralized, industrial food system. The alleged dairy-borne diseases of yesteryear occurred due to unsanitary conditions. Today we have rural electricification and thereby on-farm refrigeration, stainless steel, and hot water. What about the numerous people who have already died eating genetically engineered food?

Why in the world should entities that nobody trusts to be honest with their employees, to be honest with their customers, be trusted to be honest with our food supply? That's back to intellectual schizophrenia again.

The truth is that genetically engineered food, due to its weaker structure, is more susceptible to pathogenic invasion. It creates an inherent weakness in the cell structure's natural defenses. Just like rBGH for dairy cows stimulates mastitis and skeletal bone mass depletion, so genetically engineered plants are more susceptible to problems. Witness the multi-million dollar loss among cotton growers whose genetically engineered cotton was killed in a moderate frost--a frost that never would have affected the standard varieties. Make no mistake about it, genetically engineered foods are designed to extract the last bit of equity from the world's farmers and concentrate it in the hands of the Wall Street barons.

4. It cannot be controlled. For me this is another stand-alone nail in the coffin. How many more "Oopses" will have to occur before the world realizes that this technology cannot be handily reboxed in the laboratory?

Pollen drift and tainted, mutated derivatives are now so common in the food sector that even the organic community is admitting there probably is no such thing as a food item totally free from genetically manipulated DNA. Whatever happened to the grade school axiom: "Your freedom ends at my nose?"

The Human Genome Project started off confident that there would be 100,000 genetic pairs, based on known variables. Everyone involved in the project was shocked to learn there were only 36,000. That means a lot of hanky panky is going on as information moves along the DNA strand. This is all a major mystery. The fact is we don't have a clue what we're dealing with.

But people who we've been educated to trust are wading into this arena of glorious mystery with all the awe and reverence of a Conquistador murdering a culture and pillaging the gold into a galleon to line the coffers of an enlightened supreme potentate. Oh, the absolute debauchery of it all. It's obscene. And you thought MTV was bad.

5. It enslaves farmers to patented life forms owned by multinational corporations. If one thing represents the ultimate export of knowledge from the farm, this is it. When farmers cannot choose to save their own seed or save their own bulls, but must purchase every seed or genetic stock from a multinational corporation--all under the watchful eye of the nonpolitical, Everyman loving government watchdog bureaucracy--food choice and farming as we know it will no longer exist.

A community that can feed itself is free. A community that cannot feed itself is not. It's that simple. No, I am not a conspiratist. But I am constantly amazed at the duplicity of people to trust entities and bureaucrats that in every other arena are known to be greedy, abusive, lying miscreants. It doesn't take a rocket scientist to realize that what is the darling of a shortsighted Wall Street's financial district is not in the best interests of small farmers who love their landscapes and their neighborhoods.

How do we stop eating genetically engineered food? Very simple.

- Buy local. Buy from the farmer you know and trust. Ask to see his seed catalogue. Where does he get his bulls?

- Read Seeds of Deception and then become an activist.

- Go online and get product lists that do or do not contain genetically engineered products. Patronize the ones that do not and write letters to them telling them why you are buying their product.

The Farm Friendly Patron

Chapter 9

Be Connected

N ow it's time to swing the discussion around to you, the food buyer, the purchaser. Of course, I'm not immune to this discussion, because I buy plenty of stuff too. It's hard to grow everything. The pitch in this section is to all of us.

If I were to choose one word to summarize the kind of food buyers who patronize farm friendly fare, it would have to be "connected." All of us have to *work* at being connected because fragmentation is the easiest thing in the world.

We live in a world where professionals know more and more about less and less. Go to any symposium and you'll find a total lack of holistic thinking.   Experts consistently look at problems and opportunities only from within their area of expertise. City storm water planners can only think in terms of bigger concrete tunnels to duct water away. The city landscape crew thinks about porous, vegetative areas to act as water sinks. Very seldom do the two get together.

One of the biggest problems in the forest industry is what to do with low grade woodlots and the residues left over from timber harvest-- slash, chips, sawdust. Meanwhile, over at the cattle conference, the farmers are hearing the extension experts explaining what medications to use to keep cows healthy when they're knee deep in cold mud during the winter. On our farm, we use wood chips and sawdust as a bedding material under cheap sheds in the winter to keep the cattle warm and dry so they stay comfortable and healthy.

Our model solves the problems of both groups. But the forestry people never talk to the cattle people, and the cattle people never talk to the forestry people. Unfortunately, this scenario plays out a thousand different ways in our culture every day. It happens in testimony before Congress. I've tried multiple times to testify about agriculture issues, but I don't fit any of the pigeon holes or constituency groups they want represented. I'm too environmental for the American Farm Bureau Federation. I'm too capitalist for the environmental groups. I'm too conservative for the animal rights groups. And I'm too Christian for the liberal foodies. And I'm too environmental for the conservatives.

These disconnects are easy to spot in other people or other causes. But they are extremely hard to admit within ourselves. Each of us chooses our connections, because these define our disconnects. You can't be connected to the Wal-Mart food system and also be connected to a local food system. You can't be connected to all your high school girlfriends and have a healthy connection to your wife.

Pseudo connections are also common. Memberships in organizations in which we never participate is a good example. How many of us are "card carrying" members of a group, but we have no clue who the president is and do not regularly attend meetings? Or beyond that, how many of us think we're connected in our community, but can't name our delegate or board of supervisors' members? And then we wonder why our community has problems?

The painful reality is that many of us join environmental organizations as if that makes us connected to our landscapes. The world is full of folks who dutifully send their money to environmental groups and then patronize the very food system that is predicated on destroying the environment.

This is especially true at summer nature camps. The whole focus is reverencing nature and discovering the awesome interconnectedness in the biological world, and yet the kitchen is serving the cheapest institutional drivel stamped with a 1,500 mile transportation journey. How about that for an environmental footprint?

How many public hearings and meetings have been organized to encourage government regulations against poultry confinement houses, cattle feedlots, or pig factories? If all the attendees would focus their energy on banning those products from the school lunch program, meals on wheels, the political party fundraiser, or their civic club's menu, their efforts would probably yield faster results. The gross margins in the industrial food sector are so small that a one percent change in sales is a huge shakeup.

Probably the specific story that brought this home to me most poignantly was the <u>Humane Consumer and Producer Guide</u> published by the Humane Society of the United States and the International Alliance for Sustainable Agriculture in 1993. It was a one-inch quintuple-cross-indexed compendium of humane animal producers, organizations, restaurants, and stores. It was by far and away the most comprehensive, most attractive national directory for these kinds of products ever produced.

At the time, HSUS had 1.8 million dues paying members. Most of the entries in this directory were tiny wannabe farmers aspiring to turn their hobby into an honest salaried farming operation. These producers had the right philosophy. I do not know how many of these guides were printed, but the HSUS did not even send one to their members. Members could buy one for something like $15. Very few did.

Since I had helped formulate the guidelines, I talked to the leadership about why the directory was not more widely disseminated. It was a monumental work--and beautiful. The answer was: "too expensive." I happen to know something about the publishing business. The work in a publication is in writing, putting it together, and getting camera ready copy together. The cost is miniscule once the work is done.

Simply holding your hand on the press button and cranking off another few hundred thousand is pennies a copy compared to the pre-printing investment. Never have I been more disappointed in an effort. Instead of unleashing their 1.8 million members on the marketplace, connecting them to these fledgling humane food producers, the organization buried its work and instead invested countless millions in more regulatory efforts aimed at animal transport, auction barn standards, and a host of other things that would become obsolete if their membership got connected with alternative producers.

I have seen this kind of action by the big advocacy groups over

Be Connected

and over. It must be much easier to be against something than for something. You will not find me picketing World Trade Organization meetings or dumping manure in the parking lot at McDonald's. You will not find me dumping water in diesel log truck tanks or asking for regulations against slaughterhouses or factory farms.

If the truth be known, the vegetarians wanting tofu everything and soy milk are as disconnected from their food as the McDonald junkies. It's time to take personal responsibility and realize joining causes might assuage your guilt, but it won't do any good. Wendel Berry, icon of farm friendly food, eloquently writes about his disenchantment with the inevitable myopic, single-issue, simple-minded ranting of any large organization's leadership.

One of the most moving presentations I ever heard was also one of the shortest. I was doing a conference at the University of Guelph in Canada, a town hall type meeting with two other panelists. Each of us had a five minute opening monologue followed by questions from the students. One panelist was a high powered attorney living in a high-rise apartment in Toronto. She had an infant child. She and her husband decided the previous year to set a goal of no bar codes in their food pantry.

They spent a whole year sourcing their food. They found a local grain farmer who produced their flour. They found a nearby livestock farmer from whom they purchased beef and chicken. A local vegetable producer supplied in-season vegetables and they preserved excess to carry them through the winter. At the end of the year, they had locally sourced everything in their pantry.

She said they turned the whole experience into their recreation. Their sleuthing became both investigation, education, and entertainment. Instead of going on vacation, they headed to the country. Instead of renting videos, they headed to the country. It was all one great big satisfying, glorious adventure. When she finished her simple but profound monologue, I had chill bumps on my arms and tears in my eyes.

Here was a most unlikely candidate. A metropolitan high powered, high charging upwardly mobile white collar family. If they could do it, anybody can. What's your excuse? What's my excuse? Too many soccer games? Too many church meetings?

Holy Cows and Hog Heaven

What could possibly be more important to our family, our children, our grandchildren, our community, our world, than getting connected to our food system? Are we wanting to just rant and rave about multinational control? Would we rather scowl at untrustworthy food giants who seem to be recalling food at least once a week? Would we rather lie awake at night wondering if that tomato we ate at supper had hepatitis from a foreign sewage-fertilized field?

Or would we rather take the reigns of our own destiny, get connected to our food, enjoy eating food with a face, and know that we had done the ultimate service to our 3 trillion intestinal critters? Maybe they'd all start dancing in unison, like the Rockettes. Talk about butterflies.

Being positive is incredibly more enjoyable and fun than being negative. It gets all of us where we want to go faster. If you're waiting for the government to mandate honest food in this country, I've got news for you. It ain't gonna happen--not in your lifetime and not in mine. And the longer we wait and don't do anything about it, the shorter our lives will be. Get connected.

- Make a list of foods that can be grown locally. Obviously, it'll be hard to find bananas in Portland, Maine. This list will help you know what could be available.

- Visit the local farmers' market. They may know a producer who is not there who sells things that you can't get at the market.

- Buy a classified ad or put an ad in the local trader magazine: "Want to buy local . . . whatever. Please call . . . "

- Ask the local Cooperative Extension office what local farmers sell directly to consumers.

- Plug in the food you are looking for on the internet and see what pops up.

- Contact your state affiliate of the North American Farmers Direct Marketing Association.

Be Connected

- Join a Weston Price Foundation chapter, or start one. Ditto Slow Food. Log onto *www.eatwild.com.*

Chapter 10

Acquainted with the Kitchen

A fter getting connected to your local food system and its farm friendly producers, you'll need to get acquainted with your kitchen. This may seem incredibly elementary, but it is the next step.

The cultural shift away from the kitchen as focal point of the home is almost complete. But thanks to organizations like the Weston A. Price Foundation and Slow Food, kitchens are being rediscovered. The Star Trek idea of drinking food colored power-ade for supper and swallowing mineral pills for breakfast has ruined a lot of people. That is simply not the way our bodies are designed to be fed.

I hear on the news that many dwellings are actually being designed now without kitchens. All they have is a sink and microwave. When everything comes precooked and prepacked, essentially all you need is a trash can, microwave, and sink to wash a glass. With edible fruit leather wrappings, perhaps soon you can even pitch the trash can and get rid of the sink. When you finish your drink, you just eat the container.

Most recreation centers are already bigger than kitchens. Alright, enough of this. Farm friendly food is minimally processed. The more processing, the less percentage the farmer gets. The less the farmer's margin, the more he has to produce. The more he has to produce, the more industrial he becomes. The way to stop the vicious cycle toward ever increasing volume, waste streams, and monospeciation is to meet the farmer halfway.

Much of the processing is simply mechanical cheap labor materials handling, and that is where the farmer cannot compete. Let me give you an example just to help you understand the issue. We sell whole chickens. In the industry, cut up chickens sell for less than whole chickens. For the most part, cut up chickens are the way the industry utilizes blemished carcasses. Maybe a bird has a breast blister, broken wing, or broken leg. Mixing and matching parts allows a whole bird to be salvaged.

In the industry, an assembly line of low-paid workers uses sophisticated equipment to dice up chickens into parts at a nominal cost per bird. Remember, this is essentially a salvage operation using low-paid workers with expensive machinery.

This is why savvy food buyers who do buy at the supermarket buy whole birds--they are the least blemished ones. As a small producer, however, we have almost no blemished birds. We eat virtually all of them. We can cut up a chicken by hand, with a meat cleaver, chopping block, and knife, in about three minutes. That includes bagging, twist tying--everything. That's 20 birds per person hour. Because we respect ourselves, we set a minimum hourly labor rate of $20. At 20 birds per hour, our labor cost is $1 per bird. That doesn't count the time spent sharpening the cleaver and the knife.

In order for us to offer a cut-up bird, we would need to charge at least an additional dollar. But it goes deeper than that. We are only a family. We do not have a crew here to take over when we're done. We're tired by the time we're finished processing. Our arms are tired. Our wrists are tired. It's hard work. We don't WANT to cut up chickens. The quality of life cost kicks in and we really don't want to offer this service at ANY cost.

"Well, why don't you just hire a crew?" you ask. As soon as we do that, we have to spend time finding dependable people who will do a superior job to go with our superior product and reputation for excellence. These have to be people who are willing to work a few hours at a time less than six days per month. As soon as we hired them, we would have Occupational Safety and Health Administration regulations to follow, salaries to pay, withholding, unemployment compensation,

FICA, relationship squabbles, litigation, ad nauseum. And then we'd be wanting to triple our production, which would overrun our fields with nitrogen and stink up the neighborhood and make our farm a nasty place instead of a haven.

But, in your kitchen, even if it takes you 5 minutes to cut up that chicken, you are not doing it for a living. You don't have to think in terms of so much per hour. Do you think about return per hour when you're watching a movie? Helping your children with homework? Kissing your spouse?

To take this discussion to another level, let's talk about boneless, skinless breasts. The reason those can be offered in the industry is because the backs can be sold by the tractor trailer load to soup companies for stock. The legs and thighs can be deboned and put into chicken franks. Any retail item that creams the most delectable portion requires a huge salvage infrastructure to create marketable products from the lower quality items. The reason you can buy blemish-free cardboard-textured tomatoes in the supermarket is because most of them go to salsa, ketchup, tomato soup, and other textured uses.

Beef producers find this out quickly when their stockpile of ground beef begins to mount. Our culture does not do Brunswick Stew type cooking much anymore--it takes too long. The only reason steakhouses can exist is because fast food hamburger joints move the 60 percent of the animal that is not top grade. The cheap labor and infrastructure required to market the lower grade parts inhibits the small producer's ability to offer top grade cuts. At the end of the day, the whole animal needs to be used. Small producers who do not appreciate this concept very quickly find themselves either out of business, or trying to become an empire to create the economies of scale required by cheap labor and expensive infrastructure.

A holistic food system cannot be created with prima donna foodies who wrinkle up their noses at everything but filet mignon and blemish-free fruit. Utilizing all of the production of the whole farm is the difference between profit and loss. Often it is also the difference between an appropriate biological scale of production and an inhumane factory farm type of production model.

Farm friendly food requires that you not push the industrial template onto the producer. Otherwise it ceases to be farm friendly. Part of our responsibility as the food buyer is to keep that vicious cycle from starting.

It means you'll buy raw cheese and use your own grater to turn it into little strings. It means you'll use one evening a week to make bread. It means you'll buy a crock and grate your own cabbage to make sauerkraut. It means you'll buy apples by the bushel and use a food mill to make your own applesauce. It means you'll use your food processor and deep fryer to make your own honest-to-goodness-kids'll-die-for-'em french fries from whole potatoes you buy from the local farmer.

Now before you get your hackles up about all this time, let's do a little math. In the supermarket, you can by grade A Idaho baking potatoes for about a dime a pound. You can pick these out of a little bin at the end of the produce counter. But half an aisle is devoted to freezer cases with boxed, pre-cut microwavable french fries at 99 cents a pound - which is a ten-fold increase. That's just the cost of convenience. Look at the other costs. The potato does not require a wrapper--less landfill material. The picture-perfect fries in the box got that way because half of the potato went out in a waste stream somewhere. You should see the tractor trailer loads of potatoes and potato waste fed to confinement dairy cows in Idaho. Further inefficiencies.

The item that takes the cake for me is pre-cooked heat-and-eat boxed bacon for $20 per pound. A 4 oz. box costs $5. Don't tell me food is too expensive. Someone is buying this stuff or it wouldn't occupy shelf space. Who in the world doesn't even have enough time to cook bacon? If you're that busy, you're too busy. Get a life.

Every positive change requires an investment on our part. If you want a relationship with your children, you have to invest in them. If you want to be physically fit, you have to invest in your body. If you want to grow spiritually, you have to invest in your religion. And if you want to eat farm friendly food, you *will* have to invest in your kitchen and culinary skills. Make it your new hobby. You might surprise yourself.

I was visiting a huge egg factory farm one time and I asked what they did with all the cracks. They said these slightly cracked eggs went to a processor that dumped them into a huge press, shells and all. Of course, these shells have bits of manure and lots of chlorine on them from the wash bath. This hydraulic press pushes the eggs through a screen to separate the egg from the shell.

And that, the owner told me, is what is used in cake mixes that do not require you to add eggs. One of our little family jokes when we attend some community shindig where the dessert table has cakes is to first of all find out if it came from a mix, and then ask the baker: "Did you have to add eggs?" If she says yes, somehow, to me, that makes it a little safer. If you're going to buy a mix, make sure you have to add eggs.

I could entertain you for another hour with these industrial food vignettes, but it would only gross you out. Be assured that if the average person stepped inside any component of the industrial food system, including vegetable and fruit processing, most of us would never eat food out of the supermarket again.

And organics certainly does not offer a solution. At farmers' market I would routinely buy supermarket eggs and crack them on saucers along with our pastured eggs. This was to show the difference and create awareness among the shoppers, many of whom had never actually seen a side-by-side comparison. It was dramatic.

When organic certified eggs finally arrived in our supermarket, I started using them in these comparisons. They were much poorer than the generic store brand. I finally ran into a certifier and got the story. The sell by date is from packing, not from the day the egg was laid. In the industry, the eggs come right from the factory house onto a conveyor, through a washing machine, under a drier, across a candling booth (to check for inside abnormalities and cracks), then into a sizer and into the boxes. It's all done in the same day.

In the smaller organic industry--and I use the word "industry" on purpose--inventory glitches were playing havoc with supply so the packers were looking for a way to fudge inventory. By waiting a month to pack the eggs in their retail cartons, they were able to fudge a month on the sell by date. As a result, the organic certified eggs were much older and of poorer quality than the generic store brand at a third the price. When patrons would come by and wrinkle up their noses at those raunchy eggs, they would ask: "What's wrong with that egg?"

To which I would reply: "Oh, it's organic." You cannot legislate integrity. Period. Every trade group has its charlatans, and farmers are

Acquainted with the Kitchen

no exception. When you visit, look around, smell around, poke around, ask around, and then get that raw product under your control in your own kitchen, you build integrity into the system. Fall in love with your kitchen, and your farmer will fall in love with you.

Here are some ways to rediscover your kitchen:

- Contact the local Cooperative Extension office to see if they are conducting any food preservation classes.

- Watch for food type activities in the lifestyle section of the local newspaper.

- Ask for a Betty Crocker cookbook for next gift giving time.

- Ask a foodie friend to brainstorm a basic appliance list: mixer, slow cooker, food processor, Foley mill, pressure canner.

- Apprentice yourself to an elderly matron in your church or civic group who knows how to fully utilize a kitchen.

- Set a date next week to make one meal with raw ingredients from scratch.

- Throw out the TV to get shelf space for canned goods.

- Find a pick-your-own berry patch and then make your own jam.

Chapter 11

Eating in Sync with the Season

A fter becoming acquainted with your kitchen, the next step in farm friendly food is to synchronize your eating with seasons and availability. A corollary principle here, of course, is to preserve abundant food for when it is in short supply.

In a day when globalism offers virtually any food at any time at any place, the art of our menu being in tune with the production rhythms of our bioregion seems hopelessly and irretrievably lost. But such harmonic convergence, if I may be so irreverent as to apply that term for this discussion, is the very essence of farm friendly food.

The alternative is either to force farmers to produce anti-seasonally or to leapfrog local production in favor of far away fare. And by now you should understand all the negatives involved with dependence on far away food: lack of accountability, transportation costs, exporting food dollars out of the community, volume requirements for economies of scale, inhumane production models, concentrated volumes of byproducts like manure and processing waste.

After you make your list of available bioregional products, note the normal harvest months for each. Many farmers' markets offer spreadsheets delineating this seasonal production. Essentially these sheets are prepared with time across the top and product type down the side. Each square is one week and one variety. By coloring in the appropriate squares, anyone can see at a glance when a certain product is

Eating in Sync with the Season

in season.

Seed catalogues often do the same thing for optimal planting in various horticultural zones. Commercial produce growers routinely use such spreadsheets for their planning. It's a wonderfully simple way to express the ebb and flow of the seasons.

The whole culture of "laying food by" is such a part of my family, it is difficult to portray it to someone whose umbilical is tied to the supermarket. Let me just describe what is unthinkably routine in our family--and normative for most people until a couple of decades ago. First of all, we have a couple of chest freezers. That is primarily for meat and poultry . . . and ice cream.

I am very picky about my ice cream. I only eat it if I'm alone or with somebody. That's the only time I imbibe the stuff.

Then we have a food storage pantry for all the things we can. We normally can about 600-800 quarts of food per year. With modern pressure canners it doesn't take that long and, once sealed, this food in storage requires no energy. We even can meat and poultry. More on that in a little bit. We buy bushels of apples from an orchard and make our own applesauce. When tomatoes are rolling in from the garden, we make juice and can tomatoes. We can make salsa, ketchup, and tomato paste.

When blackberries and strawberries are in season, we make jellies, jams, and freeze quarts of berries (freezing keeps them from getting so mushy). We cut corn off the cob and freeze it on cookie sheets, then crumple it into plastic bags. When we need some, we just open the bag in the freezer and scoop out what we need for a meal.

When cabbages are ready we have a couple of 10-gallon crocks for making sauerkraut. Later in the season when cucumbers are pouring in, we reuse the crocks for making pickles--especially sweet pickles. I've always said I married Teresa for her sweet pickles. We never made them in our family but the first time I was invited to a Christmas bash with her family, her grandmother had a plate of sweet pickles. Right then and there I resolved that I could not live my life without those sweet pickles. Marrying the granddaughter seemed a close enough insurance policy. And as it turned out, it was.

The grapes ripen in late September. We pull out the juicer and begin canning our juice concentrate. We cut it half and half with water to drink. The elderberries along the river provide juice for making jelly. Grape juice is reserved for drinking.

Our basement serves as a root cellar for fall vegetables and root crops. In November, the basement is full of butternut squash, sweet potatoes, white potatoes, and cushaw squash. We mulch over late carrots in the garden and they simply become sweeter and sweeter as winter progresses. Whenever we want some we just go out and get a handful fresh out of the ground.

Laying hens are only really productive for two years. At the end of that time, we dress them and cook them in a huge roaster pan. We pick the meat off, cut it up into bite-sized chunks, and either can it or freeze it. Then when it's 5 p.m. and supper panic sets in, Chicken-a-la-King is only a few minutes away. That precooked, ready-to-go canned or frozen meat and poultry is about as handy as it gets.

Dear folks, this *laying by* behavior is considered totally normal in our family. And I confess we find it somewhat odd when a customer says they don't have a freezer. And even more so when a 40-year old mom says she has never canned anything in her life. Each of us picks our routine. For some, it's panicking at the first flakes of snow, heading to the supermarket for food. For others, it's laying food by and enjoying eating out of the larder during the winter.

Every year tons of produce gets thrown away by high quality gardeners in your neighborhood because the market does not fluctuate fast enough to meet the supply. Right before frost, tomatoes just rev into high gear and pump out sweet, gorgeous orbs. But instead of all the local folks jumping on this last gift of summer and canning all the excess for winter, the industry--including the organic industry--concentrates on how to make sure fresh tomatoes arrive on the supermarket shelves in January from 2,000 miles away. And the local tomato flood gets composted, fed to pigs, or just thrown out in heaps. The whole world could eat like kings on just the late-season flush of production from neighborhood gardens.

If all the effort expended in our culture to get fresh tomatoes on supermarket shelves in Portland, Maine in January were invested in fully utilizing the late August tomato flood, it would revolutionize our food system. In addition, it would ramp up our nutrition, recycle dollars in our local community, and free us individually and collectively from inappropriate far-away food dependency. Finally, it would in many cases be the difference between making enough to get by and making enough to romance the next generation into farming on the part of our local farmers.

Doesn't that seem more efficient than all the government schemes to subsidize this, put an easement on that, zone the other? Why is it that when I make such an all-encompassing suggestion, such a simple solution to all these huge problems that occupy reams of paper and hours of Congressional hearings, the conventional culture laughs me off as old-fashioned and irrelevant?

"Don't you know I have to get the kids to soccer practice?" "Don't you realize we have to go visit Thumper and Bambi?" Why is it that asking folks to get in touch with their food supply is inappropriate? Anyone willing to invest a week and $2,000 in frolicking with Thumper and Bambi should be willing to take a couple evenings a year and some change to get in touch with their food supply. It's part and parcel of the action plan to partake of farm friendly food.

Just so you'll understand how deep some of this seasonality can go, let me describe the egg production cycle. Little chicks hatch out and begin growing. These pullets (young female chickens) begin laying in about their twentieth week. At first, they lay what are called pullet eggs--very small. Then the size increases so that within about a month more than half the eggs are large.

The birds lay for roughly a year before molting. That is when they lose feathers, stop laying, and essentially go through a 2-4 week dormancy and rebirth period. Then, sporting a new suit of feathers and rejuvenated following the rest period, they begin another production cycle. As with nearly all biological systems, the egg production cycle follows an escalating curve early on, plateaus for a couple of months, then gradually drops to the valley during the molt period.

That is the bird's natural physiological production cycle. But other factors play a key role in the production, which, at its plateau, depending on breed, can be 5-7 eggs per week. One factor is temperature. A chicken, being a bird, has a high metabolism. Whereas a cow can ingest 10 percent of her body weight in an hour and then spend the next 23 ruminating, a chicken can only hold 1 or 2 percent of her body weight. Not only must a chicken eat frequently, but her activity level--scratching, flitting, singing--is far higher than a bovine's and therefore requires more calories per pound just to maintain body temperature. In cold weather a bird uses all the calories she can ingest just to keep warm and there aren't enough left to produce an egg.

The second factor affecting production is daylength. Light stimulates the glands that secrete the hormones that make the hen want to lay eggs. As days get shorter, production wanes. On our farm, December 21 is a red letter day because it is the solstice, the shortest day of the year. After that day, daylength increases and egg production increases until July 21, the equinox.

In a natural setting, then, peak production is in the spring and lowest production is in the fall. But culturally, demand for eggs peaks in the fall and wanes in the spring. We call it the "going back to school" syndrome. It may have something to do with the body desiring more protein heading into winter. Who knows? But every per capita consumption chart since time immemorial shows this consumption curve that peaks in November and plummets in the spring, exactly counter the normal production cycle of a chicken.

So what is a farmer to do? The industry uses lights to stimulate off-season production. I tend to shy away from this procedure because it extracts a heavier energy toll on the bird longer than normal, and that intuitively would seem to affect nutritional egg quality. The way we deal with this production drop on our farm is to start a set of pullets so that they are at their physiological peak going into the fall. In November, we bring the birds in from the pasture and put them in plastic hoophouses which warm up during the day. Although they get cold at night, the birds just snuggle together and sleep, kind of like people do in a cold bedroom.

In the daytime, the hoophouses heat up and keep the birds warm. But no matter what we do, we're always short of eggs in the fall and have plenty in the spring. But fall is when beef and pork are best. So we encourage folks to eat more meat in the fall and lay off the eggs. Eat more eggs in the spring. These seasonal fluctuations are actually fascinating when you study them, and I hope this little explanation has been interesting as well.

When we first began selling eggs to gourmet chefs, I would

76

apologize for the quality of the eggs in the winter because we couldn't keep the yolk color up when fresh grass wasn't available. During one of these conversations, the chef interrupted me and said: "Oh, it's okay. In chef's school in Switzerland we had special menus for April eggs, August eggs, and December eggs as they changed through the seasons. Some have better yolks and some have better whites, so you concentrate on recipes that capitalize on the particular quality of that month's eggs."

I stood there flabbergasted. A teenager would respond: "That is SO not me." I gained a new respect for these older cultures that place their heritage cuisine on such an honored level. Many of the restaurants we supply actually make weekly or daily menus based on what is in season. That has to be part of loving your neighbor.

When is forage fattened beef the best? In the fall. When are the deer fattest in your area? Going into winter. Once the frost has killed the flies and sweetened the grass, the cows are more comfortable than they are at any time of the year. They naturally ramp up their forage intake and backfat to get through the lean, hard winter. Beef heats you up; poultry cools you down. Spring is naturally when the chickens lay enough eggs to have extras for growing broilers. Eat chicken in the summer and beef in winter.

Historically, farmers fattened pigs on fall acorns and chestnuts. Being a monogastric, pigs enjoy a wide variety of foodstuffs, all of which are more abundant late in the season rather than in the spring. Spring diets must always come from stored inventories rather than fresh off the stalk and newly fallen to the ground. Tremendous money and effort is expended in the food system maintaining production antiseasonally.

A related issue to seasonality is the issue of eating the whole. I once had a chef ask me for 200 beef loins a year. I just looked at him and asked: "Do you know how much chuck roast that is?" Steakhouses have only been possible in our culture since the advent of the hamburger joint. Less than half the beef is top-end steaks. The rest is chuck roast and ground.

Remember, a chicken does have something besides boneless, skinless breast. The only way that can be offered in the supermarket is because the industry grinds and reconstitutes the rest, using low wage labor and high volumes to justify the sophisticated machinery to make chicken franks, lunch meat, and McNuggets. Because of the off-farm requirements for these products, they are not farm friendly. They necessarily require an industrial approach to food preparation. But you can bone out a chicken breast and cook the rest to be picked off for casseroles, freezing the broth for stock.

Tips for eating seasonally:

- Get a freezer in order to handle volume fluctuations.

- Purchase a book about food preservation and begin learning about dehydrating, canning, pickling, and smoking. Play with different techniques. Learning about this has to be as enjoyable as learning about the latest Hollywood scandal in the checkout counter tabloids. People actually buy those things, can you believe it?

- Get product-specific recipe books to see how many different ways you can fix the same thing. Entire cookbooks exist that concentrate on tomatoes, squash, eggs, beef, buffalo, squid. Enjoy.

- On Sunday afternoon, make out a menu for each day of the week. Planning ahead takes the fear out of the activity. It also reduces the temptation to panic and buy frozen pizza.

- Ask your farmer what is routinely an excess problem product and then use it. He will love you.

Chapter 12

Be Appreciative and Forgiving

T he final responsibility of a farm friendly food buyer is to be appreciative and forgiving. The notion of a farmer selling directly to the public is just gaining renewed acceptance in our culture.

Direct farm-community commerce was normative 150 years ago, but with industrialization, cheap fuel, and efficient transportation that interaction became a thing of the past. For the next 100 years farmers became the bottom rung of a food system that culminated in a supermarket.

For roughly a century farmers did not have to think about customers. They took their wares to the packing house, their animals to a sale barn, or their produce to a coop. As this cycle ran its course, farmers did not even own what they produced. It was owned by the vertical integrator, the grain elevator, or some other huge entity that contracted everything at pre-ordained low prices.

This resurgence of direct producer-consumer interaction is a new development. And it entails a new set of knowledge, a new set of skills. If you think going out into the farmers' market or the countryside to source your food, getting in touch with your kitchen, and eating seasonally are enough to upset your applecart, it is no different for the farmers you're dealing with.

Be Appreciative and Forgiving

Their heads are reeling with brand new job description requirements. Instead of just planting, watering, hoeing, and picking beans, they are now thinking about farm logos, marketing, labeling, packaging, customer lists, sanitation regulations, delivery vehicles, and product inventories. To put it in perspective, the average Tyson chicken farmer doesn't even know how to pluck and gut a chicken.

So not only does he need to learn processing skills, he also needs to learn how to greet a drive-up city slicker with a handshake and smile-- and make an invoice. It may come as a surprise to you, but most farmers have never made an invoice. They take their harvest down to the corporate buyer, he hands them a check, and that's that.

Three generations of farmers have not learned people skills, processing skills, marketing skills, or inventorying skills. Farmers have been John Deere jockeys enjoying the lonesomeness of the back 40. That's one of the things that they enjoyed most about farming--not having to deal with humanity. Peppers don't backtalk you. Cows are always happy to see you.

This became painfully apparent to me when a neighbor decided to sell sweet corn. He grew an acre of it near his house and when it was ready, took out a classified ad in the local newspaper: "Sweet corn for sale. Call 111-1111. " The first call went like this:

"Hello?"

"Hello?" Is this the place with the sweet corn?"

"Can't you read, you idiot? That's what the ad said."

The farmer told me this direct marketing didn't work because people weren't buying his corn. Obviously, it had been a long time since he took a public relations class. Editors of mainline farm publications have encouraged a disdain and mistrust toward city folks. Farmers view urbanites, and especially urban transplants, as the enemy. This has been drilled into their heads by Grandfather, who remembers the time the first non-farmer was elected to the County Board of Supervisors. It's gone downhill ever since.

Today's farmer has been raised on a steady diet of anti-consumer rhetoric since infancy. I've heard enough derogatory adjectives attached

81

to "city people" to write my own thesaurus. You would be amazed at the simmering hatred among the farming culture toward city folk. While their blood vessels pop out regaling those ignorant city folks for environmental regulations, the thought never occurs to them that their air is wafting over making the children next door nauseous--or worse.

Dear farm friendly food buyer, please understand. We farmers have not been down this path for a long time. We do not have proper infrastructure to store and process everything in neat little vacuum sealed packs with four-color logo labels. We're just trying to figure out where a T-bone comes from. We never had to know that before.

We're just trying to figure out how to leave the farm on Saturday morning to attend farmers' market. We're just trying to figure out how to keep our mushrooms cool during our delivery run to the health food store. We're trying to figure out how to keep track of you customers on the computer--for crying out loud, most of us are trying to figure out where the "on" button is for this stupid space age marvel.

Most farmers have to remodel their house to put in the computer. And you thought I was out of line for asking you to invest in a freezer and triple the size of your pantry? Try getting a farmer to create and equip a truly functional office. Now that's a trick.

I don't know how many farmers who I've encouraged to direct market their products have come to me a year later with the greatest discovery in the world: "My customers like me. They are nice people. They have good ideas. They care. They want me to succeed. I have learned so much from them." I enjoy just letting the gushing take place-- it's a catharsis for all the negativity cultivated for generations in the average farm family.

You, as a farm friendly food buyer, are part of the healing. The farmer has to heal before the land can heal. It all goes together. Every year when we send out our customer order blanks, we welcome suggestions and comments on the back. A few of our folks will take the opportunity to just put a little note of encouragement or gratitude on the back. Just an "'atta boy." Those are worth a million dollars.

The mainstream culture--and especially the USDA--treats farmers as a nonentity. Remember, more people are now in prisons than farming. The experts tell us American land is too valuable in a sophisticated economy like ours to be wasted growing food. Agricultural economics professors--paid for by your money--routinely give speeches saying that we would do better to go "offshore" with our food production, meaning it should be imported from foreign countries so we can grow more houses, Wal-Marts, and office complexes.

Environmentalists tell us farmers they should be able to dictate what to do with our land. The land that's been in our families for generations, that we've toiled on, tilled, watered, weeded, fenced, planted, hunted, and paid taxes on--that this should be taken away and placed in something called the "public trust." To us, that sounds like nothing more than blatant stealing of our most treasured possession-- even our life.

Perhaps the most formidable obstacle to direct marketing is liability. Anytime I do a marketing seminar, one of the first questions is about liability. What if a disgruntled customer sues? Underwriters who will take on the risk of direct farmer-customer sales are few and far between.

Insurance companies love the system the way it is. Many farmers are scared to death to accept that liability risk. It's fun to see articles in Gourmet Magazine or National Geographic about alternative or sustainable farmers. But knowing these folks like I do, you'd be surprised the personal agony over finding insurance, or the emotional and economic hurdles in dealing with the public. The industrial system divorces the farmer from all this responsibility. Hiding behind Wal-Mart's skirts can feel very safe.

Be assured that the new territory required of any responsible food buyer is not greater than the new territory facing a farm friendly food producer. Once the farmer decides to opt out of the industrial paradigm, he's in new territory. It's big. It can be overwhelming. In fact, it is so overwhelming that many of the pioneers have sold out to the organic empire, choosing the safety of the industrial culture once again.

But every day, new farmers are joining this exodus from the system. And they are rendezvousing with you in your exodus from Wal-Mart. As a farmer supported by people just like you, I salute you. I honor you. Your boldness, your courage to go where people have not gone for a long time, is the stuff of conviction, healing, real change. Farmers like me, one and all, share in this great homage to food buyers who accept this mantle of responsibility. In today's vernacular--you are awesome.

But so are the farmers desperate to service you with wholesome, nonindustrial food. We are cutting against the grain of our peers, our farming neighbors, our families, and our nation's agenda. We are not even considered patriotic. If we were patriotic, we'd salute Monsanto and genuflect before Aventis. Instead, we've chosen "the road less traveled. And that has made all the difference."

How can you show your farmer some gratitude and appreciation? Glad you asked:

- Be willing to take some blemished stuff. Industrial sweet corn is sprayed weekly because industrial food shoppers will freak out over one worm. Growers over spray to insure that that can never happen. Enjoy the worm--that shows it is real food. Apple scab does not affect the taste or nutrition of the apple. It's purely cosmetic. Be proud of the fact that they have some real food. Better some scab than pesticide residue.

- When the farmer needs help on a governmental level, like a zoning hearing, be a vocal supporter. Show up and help. Farmers are an incredible minority.

- Share with your farmer your favorite recipes and how you use his product. He loves your stories as much as you love your story about the farm visit.

- Promote your farmer to your friends and neighbors. Bring him additional customers to help him stay in business.

- Be quick to understand that mistakes happen. I think everyone should be in businesses for themselves for one year. All of us would develop a more forgiving spirit to those business mistakes or oversights that inevitably happen in a human system.

- Hold up your end of the bargain. If you ordered a beef, show up to pick it up and pay for it when it is ready. Be there on customer pickup day at the appointed hour. Be dependable. The farmer has been thinking about you all week--or all year. Respond with some undivided attention. Say thanks.

Farm Friendly Policy

Chapter 13

Decentralization, Bioregionalism, Globalism

We've entered the era of the global economy. Anyone who doesn't worship at the altar of globalism is branded an unpatriotic misfit. "Get with the program" according to the corporate mindset is accepting without question Wall Street's blue chip New World Order.

Allan Nation, editor of <u>Stockman Grass Farmer</u> magazine, guided an annual tour to Argentina, home of the world's premier forage fattened beef. Participants were American farmers interested in the grass-fed movement. On the last tour a couple of years ago, the U.S. Ambassador there heard about this group of Americans and invited them over to the Embassy for tea and treats. After all, it's not every day that a prestigious delegation of American farmers shows up in Argentina.

He asked them why they had come to Argentina. Nation replied: "We're here to see how they produce grassfed beef because it is more nutritious, more ecological, and more tasty than grainfed feedlot beef."

The Ambassador looked at him incredulously, then coldly informed him: "Don't you understand that the reason I am here is to get Argentina to quit grass feeding and use American grain?"

Be assured that the agenda of the powers that be is not good concerning human health, global health, and environmental health. I do not know what possesses these multinational interests to be so corrupt and against truth. Is it wrong to hate them? Is it wrong to hate Hitler? Hate is a strong word, and yet despise or disdain seems too mild for the evil promulgated on the world by these powerful interests.

During the hoof and mouth outbreak in England I hearkened back to the work of Britain's own Sir Albert Howard during his composting trials at the research station in Indore, India during the 1920s. He fed pens of cattle fresh cut grass from two different fields. One was fertilized with what he called "artificial manures"--today we would call them chemical fertilizers. The other field was fertilized with compost from the sisal, a leftover from the tea plantations.

In both corrals he placed cows infected with hoof and mouth disease. Over the course of numerous replications spanning a couple of years, all the cows in the pen fed chemically fertilized forage contracted the disease. In all the trials, not once did a cow in the corral fed compost-fertilized forage contract the disease. He proved that hoof-and-mouth, which at that time was an epizootic in India, was merely symptomatic of a nutritional deficiency. If the animals were fed biologically-fertilized forage, their immune systems would counteract the disease.

I contemplated this when I saw the great mountains of burned carcasses dotting the English countryside. I thought of the farmers whose grandfathers no doubt had selected dames and sires for these descendants. I thought of these farmers, many of whose animals were destroyed just because they were in proximity to infected ones, as government agents came with quintuplicated paperwork and the local constable to see that the dirty deed was done. I thought of the cows, quietly chewing their cuds, turning their massive sides toward the sun to stimulate their rumens with solar warmth. I thought of those sweet beasts herded up to the edge of a pit and slaughtered systematically by agents of the state who were ostensibly acting in everyone's best interests.

I thought of my own cows, selected by my father, and then me. I thought of Number 10, a red Shorthorn, Angus, Brahma cross, so gentle I can walk up to her and milk her in the field. When I come, she nuzzles up to me like a dog, asking for a scratch behind the ears, a rub along the tailbone, a gentle word. I thought about how I had built electric fences in order to mimic natural herbivore grazing patterns, how I spread tons of compost on the fields, adding trace minerals, to grow healthy, nutritious grass. I thought about how I called these cows, and they would follow me right into the corral, and how I loaded them on a trailer to go the abattoir without yelling, cussing, or beating. I thought about my dear customers, who walked in the fields and appreciated their relationship with these cows. Then I learned that our own experts were developing policy to counteract what was happening in England.

I learned that the drawing board included plans to exterminate all cows within 10 miles of any outbreak. No questions asked. No appeals. Blanket extermination. And I thought of the farmers in my community-- all honorable, all upstanding churchgoers--who are tied to the latest concoctions from the Devil's pantry. Who fill the spring air with pesticides and herbicides, who fog on systematic parasiticides to their cattle, who spread toxic fertilizer on their fields, who place steroid implants in the ears of their cows, who pen their finishing beeves up on concrete and feed them such a hot ration of corn that it destroys their stomach cilia.

And in that moment, my heart turned hot. My fists clenched. In my heart, I cried out against the inhumanity, the absolute criminal attitude of the experts, the false science. Against everything represented by the Wall Street agenda. An inaudible, desperate, panicked "No!" welled up within me. "No! You can't have Number 10. She's my sweetie. I remember the day she was born. She trusts me completely. I have cared for her as only a husbandman can. No! You can't have her."

In that moment, I resolved to die with her. In retrospect, I probably wouldn't. But so strong was the emotion, the passion, the righteous indignation within me, fueled by the utter helplessness, knowing that if that day came, no truth, no argument, no legal papers. ... . nothing could protect Number 10.

And I realized that terrorists are not just "them," they are "us." Western terrorists are more sophisticated. Our domestic terrorists do not blow up schoolhouses, they splice genes. They destroy healthy cows in the name of science. They give chemical companies free roads and dump sights. They feed brains and spinal cords to cows. They lock up pigs and chickens in concentration camps - and feed the adulterated carcasses to our nation's school children. I cannot grieve for America's pain inflicted by groups who view us as the dispenser of anti-life. Is requiring a woman to wear a burka worse than cramming pigs into crates so small that the animals can't even turn around?

Is an evil dictator worse than killing the citizenry through genetic engineering "oopses?" Is death by firing squad less democratic that death by antibiotic resistant, hyper virulent, mutated super strains of salmonella? Is denying alternative medical care more liberating than allowing choice of treatment? Is mowing the city park with machines more noble than mowing with goats or cows?

Is America better because we deny food like raw milk, raw apple cider, and unwashed eggs from entering the lips of our citizenry? Are we better because we saddle the dreams of entrepreneurial small farmers with so many regulations that most aspirants never pursue their dreams? Is emotional death better than physical death?

I grieved for the cows smoldering on burning pyres in England. I grieved for Number 10, the world she had entered. I grieved for my own lack of ability to protect her from marauding scientists, experts, and government agents who would bring the full force of tanks and cannons to make sure that she would not receive any different treatment than cows fed chemicalized feed and shot up with hormones and systemic grubicides. I grieved for the thousands of small farmers around the country who have been put out of business by government agents saying raw milk is unsafe, or backyard chicken butchering poses a danger to the community, or that a girl's kitchen-baked cinnamon rolls are a threat to the neighborhood. I grieved for the millions of food buyers denied nutritious, local, fresh, artisanal, cost-competitive food to nourish their 3 trillion intestinal critters.

I love my country. I love the freedoms here. I would rather be an American than anything else. But I am Sitting Bull. How deep can the human spirit grieve? As I listen to our leaders vow revenge on terrorists and vow to liberate oppressed nations, I wonder: "Do you care about Number 10? What will you do to protect her? What will you do to make sure truth gets a hearing? Have you no shame? Have you no care that millions of innocent cows have been slaughtered because pseudoscience refuses to believe truth? Do you not care about the children who cannot eat local, nutritious food? Does it not matter that you have terrorized thousands of farmers over their raw milk, backyard chickens, and farm kitchen pies? Do you think it's fine to kill people's spirit, to destroy dreams and opportunity, as long as you don't draw physical blood?" And I could not grieve anymore.

I went out and stroked Number 10. I talked to her. I watched her calf nuzzle up and nurse, wiggling its tail in the satisfaction of receiving warm milk. Milk that was clean and pure. Milk from biologically alive soil and grass. Milk free from chemicals and pesticides. Milk laden with immune-building properties. And as I scratched Number 10 behind the ears, felt her nuzzle her muzzle against my waist, I was overwhelmed with a sense of this place. A sense that I belonged here. A sense that my customers had journeyed to a sacred harmony.

And I knelt in complete humility and submission to the wonder of it all. I know every swale and every rock on this place. I know each animal. I know where the wet spots and dry spots are. And all that love, all that commitment, all that passion, gets passed on to my customers. Does that kind of passionate integrity exist within the agendas of Wall Street Blue Chip companies? When these stock brokers for Monsanto are wheeling and dealing, do they care about the cotton farmers who lost their crop due to an "oops" in genetic engineering? Do they care about the farmers devastated by mastitis and downer cows due to using rBGH injections on their cows? How about the pesticide-killed farm workers around the world?

In an interview with farm broadcaster Jeff Ishee at the 2004 Virginia Agriculture Summit, Dr. Michael Boehlje, professor in the Department of Agricultural Economics and an instructor in the Center for Agricultural Business programs at a leading Big-Ten university, answered a question about the future of American agriculture with this response:

"This industry now looks increasingly like a manufacturing plant rather than a farm of the past. A farmer friend of mine says 'I don't raise hogs any more. I manufacture pork. That's my business and my buildings are like an assembly line at an automobile factory. And out of the end of those buildings actually come animals, but I'm not really interested in the animals. I'm interested in the attributes those animals have. I'm interested in the chop. I'm interested in the ham. The animals are just carriers of attributes the consumer wants.' That's a different way of thinking about farming than we've thought about it in the past."

The American culture, via its multi-national corporate power structure is thrusting this paradigm on the entire world. It does not ask the pigs, the farmers, the culture if this is a good thing. It uses the power and prestige of the American economy to bully, bludgeon, and beat everyone and everything into submission to this anti-life mindset.

When my cows hurt, I hurt. When the chickens aren't happy, my heart breaks. I sleep with the animals, commune with them, stroke them, protect them.

Let me ask you something. Is that what you want from your T-bone? Is that what you want from your produce, your fruits, your nuts, your eggs? Thousands of farmers just like me have that same level of care and concern for their animals and their crops. You can join into this commitment. You will not find it at the sale barn. You will not find it at the port of entry. You will not find it at the grain elevator. You will find it in individual oases of rightness--you will find it in your bioregion.

I had a delegation from Belarussia come to visit our farm. They came down in two limousines from Washington D.C. where they were meeting with U.S. officials. Chernobyl had dropped its deadly radioactive cloud on this dairy region and the milk glowed too much to drink. Interestingly, they said the radioactivity did not affect the meat even though it settled in the mammary glands.

They were seeking to convert their region to beef production so they could feed their people. We had a delightful visit and I showed them how we produced our beef, and how we mimicked natural grazing patterns with electric fences, and how we kept them out of riparian areas and had developed gravity-flow piped water.

At the end of the visit, they agreed that our system was the answer for their country. But they didn't see how it could be implemented. They explained that the day after the millions of dollars of U.S. aid reached their country, the hotels were full of representatives from multinational corporations explaining to them how to spend this money. Dear folks, for the amount of money the U.S. taxpayers sent over there, they could have electric fenced and water-lined the entire country and produced enough beef without any tillage to feed themselves and have enough left over to export.

But instead they are floundering in the advice of powerful interests supported by millions of well-meaning stockholders and investors in this country who think U.S. aid really helps them. Welcome to globalism. Welcome to empire building. Welcome to dishonest capitalism. Did someone really have the audacity to call this "compassionate capitalism?" Yes, capitalism can be compassionate, but it sure isn't in the halls of Monsanto or Archer Daniels Midland.

One final question. People routinely ask: "Well, how do we feed New York City then? All these people can't come out into the countryside and forage for their food."

That's a fair question, and I admit that I do not have all the answers. But just because we don't have it all figured out doesn't mean we shouldn't proceed with what we do have figured out. And what we do know is that millions of food buyers, and ideally millions of farmers, can dance together in a farm friendly food system. And if everyone who could would, new opportunities would arise that we can't even conceive of yet.

Furthermore, New York City's Green Markets provide a wonderful venue for farm friendly food transactions. Ethnic operations that are directly linked to producers in the countryside are all over the place. It may take some sleuthing, some checking out, following some leads, and some time investment. But you can find farm friendly food.

Just outside the city I know scores of producers who would welcome additional customers. Getting away from all that concrete would do you good anyway. Collaborate with a few other people and take turns. If you had four families, each taking a weekly turn procuring everyone's groceries, that would be twelve trips out a year. Is that horrendous? I'm not prepared to statistically defend these trips out compared to all the tractor trailers that come in with food, and right now that is not important because efficiency never comes at the front end of a new paradigm. Creativity is inefficient.

But as more and more people join you, as the mad dash to opt out gathers momentum, new marketing and food transfer arrangements will pop up. Even now our farm is servicing several metropolitan buying clubs on a bi-monthly basis. These groups get enough volume to justify the delivery trip. And they tell me there is as much difference between our stuff and the organic supermarket as there is between the organic supermarket and Wal-Mart. Maybe you can cut down on chips and crackers for awhile.

92

Finally, I would ask a question in return: "Why should we have a New York City?" Why should I, as a clean food farmer, be responsible for maintaining something as parasitic on the landscape as a New York City? What good is it? And I'm not suggesting cities are wrong, but just because it's a big city, does it have to be bigger. Would a New York City half the size still not offer most of what it already does? Would it still not be a center for the arts and haberdashers?

A New York City half the size would be much lighter on the land. It would be less extractive of resources. It would have a smaller waste stream. It would be more amenable to change. It would still be an icon.

Cultural diversity and bioregionalism are not just hokie inventions of disenfranchised pinko environmentalists. They are terms that have defined humanity for all but the last century of American experience. Remember, cancer is growth. Cancer is bigger than the cells around it. Heritage provides soul, meaning, and moorings. The globalist enamored of big, power and techno-glitzy will eventually look for his olive tree. Hence the title and theme of Thomas Friedman's The Lexus and the Olive Tree.

Eventually, when all the thrill of the lights and the pizzazz wears off, we want to come home. But what is home? Home is where Number 10 lives. Home is where you know reality. As Friedman points out, through global communication every person is only an eighth of a second away from every other person on the planet. But that is far too separate for some very important human functions: a hug, a kiss.

Here is how to become a decentralized bioregionalist:

- Read alternative stuff. Be eclectic. TV news, both public and private, is paid for and the mouthpiece of Wall Street donors and will come from a particular slant. Check out some other stuff, both liberal and conservative. Read the reports from the Natural Resources Defense Counsel and then listen to Rush Limbaugh.

- Ask your farmer what he fears most. It will probably amaze you, but it will begin a mutually beneficial dialogue for policy positions that protect farm friendly food.

93

Chapter 14

Cheap Food

P erhaps nothing in our culture is more devastating to farm friendly food than our cheap food policy. "Pile it high and sell it cheap" is the slogan of Farmer Jack supermarkets, but it is also the policy of every politician and the average American.

- Come buy our cars. We pile them high and sell them cheaper.

- Get your drugs here. Guaranteed to be the biggest stack you've ever laid eyes on and cheap as dirt. Yes sir. We'll cure everything that aches.

- New clothes for back-to-school and prom night. We don't care how they're made, but they're here and you're bound to find something that fits. And they're cheap.

- Largest assortment of electronic devices anywhere assembled under one roof. Refrigerators to boom boxes. What a pile. It might not be good for you, and you might not need it, but the price is right. It's all cheap, cheap, cheap.

- Discount university diploma. One for everyone. We don't care how you come in or how you turn out, but you'll get a diploma and it's cheap.

Cheap Food

Can you think of any sector--any sector--of our culture that promotes its wares with a slogan like "we pile it high and sell it cheap?" Any other sector of our economy would commit suicide with such a slogan . . . except for food. Why is that? I submit that we as a culture completely disrespect the 3 trillion critters in our digestive tract that cry out for quality of life while we cram quantity of junk down their collective gullet.

Perhaps a very personal illustration will help explain agriculture economics. My Mom and Dad bought this farm in 1961 for $49,000. Today it is assessed at $500,000--a tenfold increase. In 1961, weaned beef calves brought 35 cents a pound at the local sale barn. Today they bring 90 cents--a twofold-plus increase. Corn brought $2 per bushel; today it's $3---not even a twofold increase. In 1961 diesel fuel was 15 cents a gallon; today it's $1.50--a tenfold increase. A bushel of apples sold for $8; today it sells for $12, not even a twofold increase. A moderate-sized tractor sold for $1,300; today's equivalent sells for $26,000--a twenty-fold increase.

Do you see a pattern here? Every other sector in society has risen, maybe not as fast as inflation, but at least something resembling parallel. Wages, insurance, fuel, tools, machinery. It has all increased in the neighborhood of tenfold since 1961 while commodities have only risen on average double. The policy wonks and agriculture economists tout this as progress to the efficient American farmer, and certainly some of that is true. But we've also lost hundreds of thousands of farmers and entire communities, especially in the grain belt.

One of the most interesting graphs making rounds these days in sustainable agriculture circles shows the share of the retail dollar that goes to farmers. It was about 35 cents per dollar in the 1950s and has trended down ever since until today it is pushing 9 cents and still plunging. Much of this is attributable to the fact that food is more highly processed before it reaches the consumer. The working woman has subcontracted her kitchen to Archer Daniels Midland, which means the disparity between farmgate value and consumer plate value is greater.

But it is also important to understand that during this time billions and billions of dollars in subsidies have gone to agricultural commodities to keep them from dipping even lower than they are. Who knows what the figure would be were it not for these payments? Meanwhile, the cost of inputs has risen steadily so that the lines have already crossed. Agriculture as a cultural cash cow has turned into a cultural white elephant.

This cheap food policy is only an illusion, of course. When people ask why our farm's pastured-based meat and poultry is more expensive than what is in the store, I quickly respond that it is the cheapest food around. Our food does not result in fish kills from lagoon blowouts at pig factories. Our food does not contain pathogenic bacteria that account for half of all cases of diarrhea in this country, according to the Centers for Disease Control. What is a round with Senor Diarrhea worth?

On our farm, we receive no government payments and require no regulatory oversight. Our food will not make you resistant to antibiotics if you do end up having to take some for an infection. Our poultry will not make your daughter reach puberty at 8 years old. Our farm will not necessitate government officials launching a costly investigation and litigation against us for stinking up or otherwise polluting the groundwater. We won't dump so many non-English speaking workers into the community that the school district loses 30 percent of its classroom space to English as a Second Language (ESL).

When you take all the societal and government costs associated with cheap food, you quickly realize that the really honest-priced fare is substantially higher than what is at Wal-Mart. When we buy the industrial stuff, we are simply asking society and our taxes to pick up the slack for irresponsibly priced food. We can either decide to patronize an honestly priced food system, or a dishonestly priced food system. The decision is that simple.

Perhaps the most serious ramification of a cheap food policy is that it disrespects the stewards of our natural resources. Our regional Nature Conservancy chapter has identified and is trying to protect several critical habitat areas. And while this may be noble, these areas cannot be protected without changing the way the surrounding 98 percent of the land is used. No spot on the landscape can be maintained as an island.

If the Nature Conservancy would go on a campaign to get its members to patronize local environmentally sensitive farmers with their food dollars, far more could be accomplished environmentally than

Cheap Food

saving a few tiny isolated spots of critical habitat. Seldom do these large environmental organizations even use local foods at their annual banquets and fundraisers. It's the same old institutional food pablum served at the Chamber of Commerce picnic.

It's time to make our talk and walk match. A cheap food policy tells our farmers that they are not important. Why should farmers have to work in town in order to support their hobby of farming? Does any other vocation require that? Why is it greedy for me to want the same salary as the average wage of my customer constituency?

This disrespect has resulted in rural brain drain. For a couple of generations now we have exported the best and brightest to the cities to become doctors, lawyers, engineers and accountants while the D students stayed on the farm. The stereotypical red neck tobacco spittin' trip-over-the-transmission-in-the-front-yard hillbilly hick farmer is alive and well in our culture.

Visit any school guidance office and watch how the counselors handle the bright farm kids that want to return to farming. They will be hammered and insulted for wanting such a lowly vocation. Some folks drove up to our farm the other day in their Mercedes Benz and wanted to buy some meat. I was there with my two apprentices and these immaculate, perfectly quaffed jet-set retirees came into the sales building. They were clearly well traveled, well read, articulate, and very interested in what this environmental farm was trying to do. We chatted for a few minutes and then one of the ladies couldn't stand it.

She said: "Here you are, three intelligent, gifted young men. (I appreciated her calling me a young man). What on earth would make you want to farm?"

I wanted to say: "Well, we're not really as bright as we look. We cover up our stupidity pretty well." But instead, I said: "Because it is the noblest vocation on earth and the one that ultimately controls the destiny of the planet."

This notion that only dummies farm is ubiquitous in our culture--and I didn't have to look up how to spell that word, and I didn't even use the Thesaurus. Check out the Sunday funny papers. Who are the biggest dunces? Jon Arbuckle in Garfield--farm boy. How about the doofiest guy to ever don a military uniform? Zero, in Beetle Bailey. As a society we have dishonored and trashed our farmers to the point where nobody with confidence or brains wants to do it.

And the collective sucking sound you hear in rural America, as a result of this attitude, is the draining of brains, creativity, and can-do attitudes among those who are entrusted to grow our food. Is it any wonder farmers don't think? Is it any wonder they don't make good business decisions? Is it any wonder they sign their farms away in multinational scheme after multinational scheme?

Demographers tell us that in the next 15 years nearly 70 percent of American's farmland will change hands because the median age of the American farmer is now nearly 60 years old. Because of this cheap food policy, most farm children do not want to continue farming. What will happen to that land? What will happen to our capacity as a nation to feed ourselves?

I pray that because of this book, a new awareness, and a new loyalty to honestly priced food from respected farmers will create a passionate desire in the hearts of thousands and thousands of young people to *nurture* this land. To love it like a native. And to offer sustenance to their communities with healing food . . . with farm friendly food.

Finally, cheap food is extremely subjective. I had a woman come by my farmers' market stand the other day sipping on a can of soda she had just extracted from a nearby vending machine for the paltry sum of 75 cents. By studying her hairdo I surmised that she had just been to see the beautician. She looked at my eggs and snorted: "What? Two dollars a dozen! I'd never pay that for eggs!"

I felt like saying: "Ma'am (actually, I must confess that I didn't feel like saying "ma'am") there is more nutrition in ONE of my eggs than there is in a tractor load of those 75 cent sodas."

What are the largest food corporations in the world? Coca-Cola. Hershey's. Taco Bell. McDonalds. Goodness, these outfits are not in the food business. They are in the recreation and entertainment business. Nobody needs candy, McDonald's or Coca-Cola. If those outfits closed up overnight and all their employees, all their janitors, all their mechanics, all their advertising executives became farm friendly food producers, would we as a culture be richer or poorer? I submit that we would be richer, and we would be loved by many cultures that currently hate us for exporting this type of junk around the globe.

The trend in every corporate board room is to push down the input costs, to play vendor against vendor. This is true in organics as well as anywhere else. And with Wall Street outfits snarfing up organic cooperatives every day, compromises will be made to undifferentiate the superior qualities that used to define these products. The commoditization of organics will defeat it. But that adulteration of organics simply creates and insures more opportunity for true-blue bioregional producers.

It deeply saddens me to go into the average health food store and note that 95 percent of what is on the shelves comes from just as far away, is packed the same way, and often is picked and processed by the same socially unjust labor pool as the Wal-Mart counterparts. Are organic Twinkies really what we're after?

Or is it honest food at an honest price? Is it accountability? Is it respect that only comes when two people lock eyes? Each of us food buyers has the power to instill pride in our producers. We can reverse this cultural attitude in our community with our network of farmers. Whether it's demanding that our hole-in-the-wall health food store stock local stuff, or venturing out beyond the sidewalks to source our own food, we can multiply the power of one to create a farm friendly food system.

Here are some ideas for eliminating the cheap food policy.

- Eliminate all agricultural subsidies that simply steal from taxpayers to cover the sins of a boneheaded food system. Why should vegetarians pay for mad cow coverups? Why should raw cow milk lovers subsidize soymilk?

- Buy from farmers who set their prices. He who sets the price controls the show.

- Make sure any organization of which you are a member uses nonindustrial food at its next meal function. That includes civic clubs, PTA, and especially school lunches.

- Ask your health food store to host a local source fair. Local farmers can come and offer their wares. Some health food stores actually offer their facade as pickup points for buying groups. A slight commission can be collected but it routinely generates more business for the store and gives it the air of a community clean food centerpiece. A real public relations buzz.

- Give this book to all your friends.

Chapter 15

Regulation

I 'd like you to take a moment to answer a question for me: What is the biggest impediment to your being able to eat farm friendly food?

In case you're not clear about what I'm asking, I'll rephrase it: What is the biggest hurdle to you being able to choose what to feed your 3 trillion intestinal workers?

Think about that a minute. Look up from this page and take a deep breath. Answer it for me.

Now let me see if I can guess what you're most likely to say:

- Not enough organic supermarkets; or Wal-Mart won't carry farm friendly food.

- Not enough USDA-sponsored research into farm friendly production methods.

- Not enough government grants for alternative programs and thinking.

- People are too busy to care.

Regulation

- TV commercials that push junk food.

- Farm friendly food is too expensive.

- Poverty.

- Republicans

- Democrats

- Capitalists

- Environmentalists

- The Confederacy

Okay, we'll cut this, but I think at least at the beginning I was in the ballpark on the most common ones. The one I submit is not on the list because I do not hear the sustainable, organic, alternative agriculture community dealing with this at all. Most are lobbying for more government intervention, more public money, and more bureaucratic involvement.

For the record, here is my answer: government regulations that deny farmers and food buyers from doing business without passing the transaction through a gauntlet of prohibitive requirements. In short: government regulation.

Consider the following three points:

1. You can go deer hunting, shoot a deer on a 70 degree day, toss it on your gas guzzler as a hood ornament and parade around town all afternoon before returning to the back stoop to dice it up and feed it to your buddies and their children anyway you choose, but you can't dress a beef steer and sell one T-bone to your uncle. For Democrats, this whole scene is rife with horror: guns, hunting, gas hog vehicles, self-gratification, having fun. Oops, I went too far. For the Republicans, this whole scene is the essence of Americana: sports, home, freedom, and good ole boys.

2. You can eat sushi in a landlocked state and buy it from

anybody, but you can't buy raw milk from a neighbor's cow even when you stand and watch it being milked.

3. Scallions can be washed in non-potable water and sold in fast food restaurants, but a neighbor can't sell you canned tomatoes at the farmers' market.

The bottom line for me is this: If you want to come to my farm, ask around, look around, smell around, and make a voluntary informed choice to patronize my product, it's none of the government's business. Period. But how did we get to the point where such sensible freedom would be denied in the land of the free and the home of the brave?

Shortly after 1900 when Upton Sinclair wrote The Jungle that exposed the filth of the large Chicago slaughterhouses, the public demanded government intervention. "We need to regulate those nasty businesses," was the cry on the public's lips.

A little historical perspective is in order. Within six months of that book coming out, beef consumption in this country dropped-- depending on what historian you read--30-50 percent. Question: How long would the beef industry accept that drop without making major changes? Answer: Not long.

Private certifying agencies would have sprung up, something like Underwriters' Laboratories for electric cords. Journalists would have been crawling all over those companies, checking things out and keeping the pressure on.

For sure, many people reverted to small community abattoirs rather than buying in the glitzy town butcher shop. Grocery stores would have banded together and hired inspectors to go certify cleanliness so that retailers could assure their patrons that their particular meat stream was safe.

A drop of that magnitude certainly would have gotten the attention of the industry and it would have adjusted accordingly. But no, an impatient consumer mob demanded government intervention. And what we got was the U.S. Food Safety and Inspection Service. Like so many government programs, started sincerely and with all good intentions, today these Nazis canvass the countryside terrorizing anyone who would dare sell a glass of raw milk to their mother without official government approval.

These government agents have tried to shut down our farm several times, but we have always enlisted the help of our politicians and thwarted these attacks. We have been blessed so far to withstand these attacks. But thousands of other small farmers have been intimidated into going out of business.

The problem is that these regulations are regulations of system and not quality. Let me share one of our own exchanges with you so you can see how these seemingly consumer-protective regulations actually get implemented outside the beltway.

Here at Polyface, we process poultry in an open-air facility a few days a month. Government inspectors came and told us that this procedure was inherently unsanitary. We had our chickens cultured for exterior bacteria in a laboratory that measured the results in colony forming units (cfu) per milliliter to the second permutation. I already don't understand what I said; all I'm telling you is what is on the report.

The lab cultured supermarket chickens at the same time, for comparison. The supermarket birds averaged 3,600 cfu/ml. and ours averaged 133 cfu/ml. That's a factor of 2,500 percent, or 25 times fewer bacteria. And yet these agents said that because we did not have walls on our processing shed, it was inherently unsanitary. They said if one fly entered the shed and landed on a carcass, that chicken would be considered unsanitary and adulterated.

It didn't matter that our chickens were 25 times cleaner. I encouraged them to take their own sample. Guess what? They had no thresholds! They had no empirical scientific standards! All they had was a subjective notion that open-air processing was inherently unclean, end of discussion.

They said the regulations required that we have walls. I asked them to show it to me in the law. They found a section that said: "Doors and windows must be screened." They argued that clearly the formulators of the code assumed that the facility would have walls.

I responded that they could infer nothing of the kind. It simply said that if you did have walls, access openings had to be screened. Since we didn't have any doors or windows, screening was unnecessary.

Holy Cows and Hog Heaven

I offered to mount a door on a pole and put a screen in it if that would make them happy. They didn't appreciate my humor.

I finally asked them: "What would I need to pass your approval?"

They said the first thing we would need is a bathroom. I asked them what for. They said: "For your employees."

I said: "Look, gentlemen, we don't have any employees. We're just family here. This shed is 50 feet from our house and 50 feet from mom's house. Each house has two bathrooms. We've got four bathrooms within 50 feet of this shed. And for that matter, if I have to go Number One, I can just step around on the other side of the tractor. What are you going to do about that?"

Folks, these kinds of exchanges happen thousands of times all across our land, and the result is that you and I cannot access the kind of food we want. They effectively eliminate farmers from being able to access their neighbors with alternative food.

In the real world, consumers don't sit around in focus groups and ask for new products; entrepreneurs dream up new products and then market them. In the mid-1960s a group of people sitting around at a Sunday church picnic didn't all of a sudden come to the conclusion that what was missing at the local toy store was something called a Hula-Hoop. No, somebody somewhere started fooling around with a bicycle rim or something and conceived of the Hula-Hoop idea. He then sought funding, a manufacturing facility, made some phone calls, and introduced this new product to the market.

That is the way new products arrive in the marketplace. And if regulations keep them from arriving, potential buyers do not have a clue what they are missing. And that is the real tragedy of where we've come in this country. The average food buyer believes a full spectrum of choice is in front of her when it is not. It is actually half a spectrum because many of the options that could be offered do not exist due to these capricious government requirements.

I cannot sell a neighbor bacon from my pig unless that pig is slaughtered at a government approved facility. But a slaughterhouse is prohibited in agriculturally zoned land. The very facility required to get you a pound of bacon is prohibited on my farm. As a result, I transport the pig up the interstate, out of the county, to an approved facility. This adds to the consternation of the pig and the congestion of the already clogged highway.

We take the pig to the slaughterhouse the evening before so its meat toughening adrenalins can settle down overnight. Meanwhile, other people are unloading their animals of various and sundry dubious extraction into the holding area in pens adjacent to my clean pigs. The next day, completely out of my sight and beyond my control, my pigs are slaughtered by hirelings, some of whom speak my language and some of whom do not. Then the carcass is pushed into a giant refrigerator with many other carcasses.

A couple of days later, my hog is removed for cutting up by a crew of people wearing long coats with deep pockets--all completely removed from my control or oversight. Then a couple of days later I get to enjoy another trip back up the same clogged interstate to retrieve my pork.

But wait a minute. The bacon must be cured. I can't bring back the fresh pork sides and cure them at my farm in a smokehouse or curing room like people do all over the world--and used to do in this country until recent times. No, this side meat gets picked up by another outfit to be transported over the interstate to another inspected curing facility. A totally new set of hirelings completely out of my oversight cures the bacon, cuts it, and shrink wraps it. Then the bacon gets another ride over the same interstate back to the original slaughterhouse, where I get to ride up the interstate again and pick up the cured parts of my original hogs.

I could cure the bacon on our farm if I had a registered retail store. But a retail store is also prohibited in an agricultural zone. Even if it were permitted, it would need approved parking area, public restrooms with approved septic systems, handicapped access and parking, and commercial road access with appropriate sight distances.

But here's the catch. If a product leaves a farm for further processing and then is returned to the farm for sale, it falls under the definition of "manufactured product." It is illegal to sell a manufactured product from a farm. So now that I have jumped through all the hoops just to get my neighbor a pound of bacon, it's illegal to sell it to him because it is a manufactured product.

Folks, I am not making this up. I could go on and on for a day with these stories (someday I'll write a book about them), but I hope you are now convinced that these regulations limit food freedom big time. Most farmers simply throw up their hands and don't even try. Many, many farmers have quit. Our county used to have several community canneries and a dozen abattoirs. Now they are all but gone. But never fear, we have Wal-Mart. Isn't that sweet consolation?

Public policy action steps:

- Constitutional amendment: Right to sell from the farm free of government regulation.

- Objective standards for pathogenicity. If I can make cheese in my kitchen sink that meets the pathogen standard, I should be able to do so.

- Allow food buyers to accept responsibility for the risk of their own decision.

- Everybody just begin defying the law so that inspectors all die of a heart attack trying to keep up with putting everyone out of business. Since the government is broke and can't afford to replace these folks, we'll win by default.

Chapter 16

Preserving Embryonic Entrepreneurs

I can hear Ralph Naderites and consumer advocacy types responding, after the previous chapter: "Why don't you just find a spot in a commercially zoned area and put in an inspected curing facility, slaughterhouse, etc., and just get over it?"

Good question. Let me tell you why I can't just "get over it."

I'll start with an example. New regulations coming down on cider makers are requiring pasteurization. Never mind that it destroys a lot of the nutrition, affects taste, or any number of other things. Pasteurization itself is not a huge deal. But the little itty bitty catch to this is that the government approved pasteurizers for this process cost-- depending on who you ask--between $30,000 and $50,000.

That's one thing if you are a plant doing millions of gallons of cider. It's quite another thing if you're a 10-acre orchard--or less-- squeezing some for your neighbors. In most cases, custom processing is not an option, or at least not an economical one.

Harking back to the previous chapter and my story about our bacon's travels, even if it were legal to sell at the farm, all of this custom processing adds $3 per pound. That means when you buy a pound of bacon from us at $6, $3 of it goes straight out the back door to pay invoices from the processors and custom curing. From what is left, we have to pay for the piggies we bought from the farrowing guy, the feed

110

the pigs ate, infrastructure to raise the pigs, labor to care for the pigs, and all those miles up and down the interstate in trailers and vehicles suited to the task.

The issue is one of scale. When every pound of bacon and every T-bone steak have to be wrapped in a $1 million quintuple-permitted, agricultural-zone prohibited facility, the small guy is out. Producing on a farm friendly scale can't capitalize the infrastructural overhead.

If you read the stories of Bob Evans, Jimmy Dean, Frank Perdue, Don Tyson and other empire magnates, you find very humble beginnings. I've met Bob Evans several times and he tells great stories about selling sausage from the tailgate of his pickup truck half a century ago.

All of these folks were visionaries with ambition and creative, efficient ideas. But each one started small and grew, financing the additional infrastructure mortar and stainless steel with product volume. But if they had been required to build a $1 million facility before offering the first chicken or the first pound of sausage, they never would have been able to bring their new entrepreneurial marketing scheme, and the advantages of their product, to the marketplace.

If we do not preserve the freedom for embryonic entrepreneurs to access the marketplace today, just as we did for these earlier innovators, tomorrow's innovators will birth nothing but stillborn products and miscarried ideas, especially if each prototype requires a megalithic investment.

Why has ecommerce exploded? Because anyone, in their home, on their already-owned computer, can start a business. What if ecommerce had been inspected and certified by government agents who required that each access port be in a commercial district with a certain sophisticated computer capability? How many would-be ecommerce folks would have offered their new product or idea to the world? Very few.

On the ragged edge of paradigmatic disequilibrium is a freedom to jump in and out without destroying your whole life. As the long term risks of exposing yourself to the ragged edge escalate, fewer and fewer people will jump in. That limits innovation and creativity.

Holy Cows and Hog Heaven

Giant oak trees do not propagate themselves by dropping 20 ft. babies out of their tops. They propagate from tiny acorns, because that is the smallest viable structure of the parent. Because it is small, it can be carried by animals to new locations, buoyed on water to be deposited on a bank downstream, or it can simply roll down a hill to a fertile spot. Its size is its strength.

Nobody knows how many hundreds of heritage pickle makers have not been able to share their skill and bounty with their neighbors because one jar required a $20,000 inspected kitchen. Nobody knows how many artisinal backyard potato soup makers have never accessed the dream of turning their craft into a part-time income because the first bowl required 10 meetings with bureaucrats all determined to protect their turf who keep passing the buck to someone else.

I was in Ohio doing a marketing presentation for the Ohio Ecological Food and Farming Association annual meeting when the rBGH issue was at its height. This is the patented hormone injected into cows to make them produce more milk. The organic community, consumer advocacy groups, and environmentalists were going apoplectic over this procedure and the milk not being labeled as containing the hormone.

I asked this roomful of a hundred folks: "If you could milk 10 cows on your 25 acre farmette and net $15,000 per year selling milk to your neighbors at retail prices, how many of you would do it?" Every hand in the room went up. If all the effort expended to fight rBGH had been focused on freeing up entrepreneurship which is alive and well in the countryside, unleashing all these folks and the farmette production on the marketplace, rBGH would become a nonissue. We small producers would run the big boys out of business. Doesn't this difference in mindset make sense?

It's a lot easier to be against something than for something. Being against something does not really require any alternatives, or in debate terminology, a plan. In interscholastic debate competition, an affirmative team wanting to change the system must not only offer a compelling indictment of the current system, but must also offer an alternative plan. If the negative defeats either part, the affirmative loses.

And that is one of the main reasons for this book. Your farmer, or your farmers' market, CSA, buying club, local-patronizing health food

112

store--all represent venues that provide creative alternatives to the myriad issues harangued about by environmentalists, libertarians, free enterprisers, consumer advocates, and economic development specialists.

Preserving embryonic market access is the key to creating the solutions to today's problems. I realize it may be heretical to believe that real solutions arise out of common people thinking uncommonly. A healthy portion of our culture thinks that the only fount of solutions comes from the government. But government solutions by definition have to satisfy 51 percent of the people--at least in a representative form of government like ours. This level of popular endorsement inherently eliminates government solutions as being true cutting edge.

Every great solution was laughed at by the mainstream. Every great idea was initially termed lunacy. I realize that many of you liberals who never saw a regulation you didn't like may be suffering a stroke right now, not used to an environmentalist sounding like a free marketer, but I hope this discussion will find a resting place in your heart to at least consider a wider view.

Government programs almost never solve the problems they were founded to solve. But the power of one, the power of the people, is real. The power of one really great idea is immeasurable. It is the freedom to pursue that one idea that has been the strength of this country. "Yankee ingenuity" is powerful because it's allowed to see the light of day.

The fact is that in many sectors of our economy, we make concessions for small operators. In most states, you can keep two or three children in your home without being subject to day care regulations.. Why? Because a person keeping that few children in their home will be able to watch them closer, reducing the need for safety devices. Because the parents will have a relationship with the child sitter. Because sanitation is easier with two or three children than it is with 30. This is a reasonable and justified exemption to daycare regulations.

A similar one involves elderly care. Again, in most areas of the country, you can keep two or three elderly folks in your home, as a business, without adhering to nursing home regulations. The reasons are the same as for the day care. And yet in neither of these cases are people being abused or uncared for. The stories of abuse or neglect are 90 percent from accredited, licensed, credentialed, government regulated facilities. Smallness carries numerous safeguards inherent in the business.

In many states, uninspected or unlicensed farm vehicles may be used on public roads as long as they are transporting farm products and aren't more than 40 miles from the farm. Farmers who use this exception do not go often, far, or fast, and are virtually never involved in automobile accidents. This is a wonderful concession to farmers who make an occasional trip somewhere and can't afford all the bells and whistles required to maintain a commercial vehicle driven by employees at all hours of the day or night.

Regulations must be appropriate to scale. Bureaucrats love to say "we must have a level playing field." In other words, it's not fair for me to bake a cake in my home kitchen and sell it to my mother-in-law down the street if the Wal-Mart birthday cake shop needs a floor drain, impermeable washable walls, separate ovens, foot-operated hand sinks, and whatever else a commercial outfit would use.

This would be akin to telling our young people: "Sure, we want you to play football. But since professionals need an NFL stadium in which to play, you boys can't play in the churchyard this afternoon; you can only play in a properly officiated game at the 60,000-seat stadium." Isn't that crazy?

Bottom line: food buyers are denied freedom to buy farm friendly food because of capricious regulations that discriminate against this kind of food.

Solution:

- Enact farmgate freedom-to-sell legislation.

- Realize that most government solutions hurt instead of help.

- Begin buying bootleg cider and bacon. It's better and it's fun.

Chapter 17

Food Safety

N ow that we've laid the groundwork in the previous chapters, let's tackle the food safety issue. Even though the sense of the previous four chapters is certainly easy to follow, many people choke at this point: "But what about all the dirty farmers? Not everyone is as conscientious as you. We can't just let these folks sell their stuff to the public. Someone might be harmed."

In Virginia, our Commissioner of Agriculture told me at a hearing that "raw milk is as dangerous as moonshine." One of his deputies told me the same day that my notion of letting individual food buyers who wanted to make informed, voluntary decisions to opt out of government-sanctioned food "bordered on criminal."

At another hearing, our Commissioner took me aside and told me: "You must understand that I am responsible for every morsel of food that goes into the mouth of every citizen of the Commonwealth." You nonVirginians must understand that we are not a lowly state here, we are a *commonwealth*. Aren't you jealous? You should be.

I responded to him: "If that is true and you believe it, you couldn't sleep at night. And the truth is it's an asinine responsibility anyway." Needless to say, we don't go fishing together.

I have several responses to this food safety question. Let's go through them systematically.

116

Food Safety

1. Food safety is subjective. To these bureaucrats, irradiation, genetic engineering, hog factories, rBGH milk, poultry chlorine baths, pasteurization, pesticides, herbicides, chemical fertilizers, and Wal-Mart are safe. Each of us chooses what we believe is safe, within our sphere of information.

For example, I don't think it's safe to bungee jump. Those of you who have would scoff at me for being afraid of it. If you want to bungee jump, I think that's fine. And if I don't, I hope that's okay with you.

For that matter, I think a vegetarian diet is harming a lot of people--it's not safe for most folks. But if you want to do it, that's okay with me. By the same token, a fast food diet, I believe, is extremely unsafe. But not to these government agents. They throw around "science" as if it's objective and "safe" as if it's objective. Neither term is objective. We need to get that through our collective heads.

I decide, and you decide, where to place our faith in safety. It all comes down to a matter of who we will trust. Anyone who believes the government watchdog agencies have no political agenda and are trustworthy is living with their head in the sand. If you trust the government, then please patronize government-sanctioned food. But to require me to trust the government with my food is Nazi tyranny.

2. Paranoia is easy, but seldom justified. I have listened to countless liberals and bureaucrats brainstorm all the terrible things that would happen if people were free to opt out of the government-sanctioned industrial food system. Oh, there will be outbreaks of undulant fever from raw milk and deaths from chicken bacteria and disease from dirt left on carrots. Oh, it will be the end of civilization as we know it--like Y2K. Remember that?

We've homeschooled both of our children. They're up and gone now. But 20 years ago, I remember the dire predictions from the education establishment when the pioneers in the movement, many speaking and writing from prison, were preaching freedom of educational choice. Oh, these experts said, we'd have negligent parents who would raise ignorant misfits. Oh, these children will grow up unsocialized and they will fill our mental institutions because they won't be able to cope with the real world.

Holy Cows and Hog Heaven

What has actually happened? Some astute, wise colleges are now asking for homeschoolers. Who keeps winning the national spelling bee? Who gets elected to the state 4-H cabinet? Who occupies leadership positions in every sector of our society? Homeschoolers. Yes, a few isolated cases of neglect or abuse have surfaced, but they've been noteworthy due to being exceptions rather than normative.

The reality is that farmers who choose not to sell through the industrial channels inherently are more careful about product quality. Irradiation is simply a wonderful way to allow people to eat sterile poop. Doesn't that make you feel good? Farmers closely linked to their clientele do not hide behind high-powered Philadelphia lawyers on retainer to act as a veil of protection from litigious consumers.

Farm friendly food is open, out front, and vulnerable. The inherent vulnerability provides integrity to the system that the industrial counterpart can never have. Besides, who is being harmed by food these days? It's not the folks eating nonindustrial fare, that's for sure. The food recalls and pathogen problems have come not from small producers, but from government-approved facilities.

3. The "farmers might be dirty" view assumes that "bureaucrats are never dirty." I will never grant that, as a whole, bureaucrats are more trustworthy than farmers. I think bureaucrats and their corporate fraternity are more conniving, more political, more arrogant, and certainly more uncharitable than any group of farmers I know--even the ones that belong to the Farm Bureau Federation.

As a societal subculture, you won't find a better bunch of people than farmers. Of course there are bad eggs. But to say that as a whole they are more evil than bureaucrats is not an assumption that I will entertain for a moment. And yet that is what is philosophically demanded of anyone who believes we need bureaucrats to protect us from these bad farmers.

The worst farmers are the ones who hide behind the corporate skirts. The ones who know that when their pig factory manure lagoon springs a leak and pollutes a few miles of river, that corporate lawyers will be there to protect them. The ones to fear are not the farm friendly operators marketing through short channels to their clients.

Food Safety

4. It's not about food safety. If it were, you couldn't give it away. All these prohibited foods, from homemade tomato sauce to raw milk to backyard bologna, can be given away to your heart's content.

A 10-year-old girl can make all the cakes she wants to in the home kitchen and donate them to the local fire department's Friday night bingo prizes to be given to people she's never seen or heard of. These folks can take these cakes home and even feed them to their children-- imagine that. But if one of those winners comes to the farm to buy one, she can't sell it.

I can go shoot a deer on a 70-degree November day, drag it through the dirt and leaves for two hours, throw it on the hood of a pickup and drive, in the blazing sun, to a neighborhood abattoir, then give the meat to all the neighborhood children. Or it can go to the Hunters for the Hungry program to feed the needy. But if I sell one pound of it, I'm a criminal.

The entire food safety issue is a smokescreen invented by bureaucrats and academic eggheads, not to mention corporate executives, who fear a little competition or a little loss of power. It's not about food safety; it's about eliminating competition by denying market access.

In every other sector of things that are inherently dangerous to the "general welfare," a prohibition exists on both buying and selling the product. Illegal drugs cannot be sold or purchased. But on food, the prohibition is only on the seller, not the buyer. You can acquire these dangerous foods all you want and feed them to your children and your neighbors; I just can't sell them to you. Well, if this food is so all-fired dangerous, why are you free to buy it and use it? It's not about safety.

5. Historical food safety problems are archaic. You will hear scientists and experts allege all sorts of food-caused diseases from yesteryear. First of all, virtually all of these were breaches of natural templates that are inherently part of a farm friendly food system.

Things like feeding kitchen wastes to cows around New York City. Or feeding raw meat leftovers from restaurants to pigs. Or fertilizing vegetables with raw human sewage. Or letting milk sit out in the hot sun for two hours before it was picked up by mule-drawn wagon to be carted to town for processing.

Holy Cows and Hog Heaven

Okay, some of these things happened. But today we have much more information about bacteria and how it multiplies. We have rural electrification, for crying out loud. We have stainless steel, cheap digital memory-chip thermometers. We have filters and on-demand hot water with soap if we want it. We have on-farm walk-in coolers, electric fence, and grassfed livestock. We have seaweed-fish emulsion foliars with excellent surfactants and magnetized sprayers.

Most of us farmers even take a bath more than once a week now. Fancy that. Just because a historical reality existed does not mean the same conditions exist or persist to reproduce it--unless the same violations occur. And because of the relationships farm friendly food inherently creates, I do not believe that these same breeches of basic sanitation and husbandry will likely be repeated. Except in feedlots, pig factories, and Archers Daniel Midland. Oh, that's right, they have irradiation to make it all okay. Forgot about that little insurance policy.

6. The freedom to choose unwisely is the only way to create an informed food buyer. Stick with me on this one a little bit. How do you get your children to make responsible decisions?

Do you do it by making all their decisions for them? Do you do it by making them completely dependent on your approval before they act? Of course not. You create responsible young people by gradually backing off your oversight of their decisions. When they face the consequences of their decisions, they become more and more informed about who they are, what they want, their value system.

None of us becomes informed about things for which we are not responsible. If someone else is responsible, we usually don't worry ourselves over that subject; we devote our attention to learning about the subject for which we are responsible.

Now I ask: "Who wants an informed food buyer? How do you create an informed food buyer?" You should be ahead of me on this one. It's not that difficult. You create an informed food buyer by giving her some responsibility for her decisions. As a culture, we have governmentally-hovered over the food system for so long that the average person doesn't even think about their food. If it's in the grocery store, it's safe. If it has that government inspected label on it, it's okay.

Food Safety

This has created an incredibly ignorant food buyer. I don't know how many articles there have been in recent years about feeding chicken manure to cows, but the average person on the street is incredulous when you mention it to her. Post mad cow outbreak in Washington State in 2003, the world was abuzz over this new-found revelation that "downer" cows were routinely ending up in hamburger.

Whenever we give over responsibility to someone else, it's out of sight, out of mind and we devote our attention to other things. For those people who want to continue being uninformed, Wal-Mart is there. Go buy your food there. But for the folks who want to take responsibility, who want to make informed decisions, freedom to patronize an unsafe producer is the stimulant to become an expert on that subject.

You cannot preserve freedom to choose creatively nonstandard alternatives by denying the freedom to make a bad choice. If only the government proscribes what's available in order to keep people from being able to make bad choices, it will also keep them from being able to make positive choices. If the government says only square boxes can be sold, who can sell triangular ones or round ones?

7. No risk-free environment exists. The truth is that our government-sanctioned food system is woefully out of whack. It is destroying the environment, destroying the dignity of plants and animals, destroying the dignity of farmers. It is an economic nightmare, requiring an army of bureaucrats to police industrial waste streams and huge revenues to indemnify the industries for self-induced epizootics like mad cow and avian influenza.

A zero tolerance for risk, as numerous food safety officials have suggested, is pedantic prattle. Life is risky--you can die from it. The risk of eating at McDonald's every day is surely as great as the risk of eating from your own kitchen a staple of non-chemical grown nearby farmer produced food. A risk-free environment simply does not exist this side of eternity.

What amazes me is the people who use this standard are exhibiting the most risky philosophy of all. They trust the government more than farmers. They trust industry more than farmer's market masters. They are willing to risk their families on the integrity of genetic engineers and irradiation, but not compost and farm kitchens. Who is exhibiting the risky behavior here? It sure isn't farm friendly food buyers.

8. Empirical standards probably won't work. The Ralph Naderites have suggested testing for bacteria in slaughterhouses. This sounds great on the surface. The only problem is that the test costs $300.

If you're a Tyson processing plant handling $1 million worth of product a day, this test fee is a drop in the bucket. But if you're a farm friendly pastured poultry producer handing $1,000 worth of product a day, this fee just put you out of business. This is the real world of how sincere-sounding regulations actually end up helping the industry and hurting the farm friendly producer.

At the other end of the spectrum, conservatives tend to applaud efforts to put the costs onto industry rather than the taxpayers. But the cost overhead drives out the small producer every time. If the public demands it, the public should pay for it, period.

The other concern is the lack of integrity in the government testing laboratories. Numerous stories have come out about technicians purposely or negligently mishandling samples. One of the most egregious was a cheese sample that was dropped on the floor of the lab but not discarded as a sample. When pathogen tests came back positive, only the quick thinking of the cheese maker, who sent a sample to an independent lab with a clean result, averted a disaster.

If the government can't be trusted to choose our religion, why should it be trusted to choose our food? It all boils down to freedom of choice. Think about the freedoms we enjoy in this country. Freedom to homeschool. Freedom to hunt. Freedom to eat irradiated salami and feed it to our children. Freedom to abort human babies. Freedom to pump methyl bromide into strawberry beds.

What's wrong with freedom to choose our own food? Why is that such a Satanic notion? Make no mistake about it, many, many people in our society view this notion as the ultimate evil thought. The liberals can't bear to think that free enterprise just might have the answer and businesses--even small farm businesses--can be trusted. The conservatives can't bear to see the Wall Street power base eroded.

Food Safety

But you and I walk to the beat of a different drummer. We don't have to be beholden to anybody's agenda except the agenda for truth and righteousness. We can choose wisely. Let's choose farm friendly food.

Don't forget:

- Safety is ultimately about faith--who you will trust.

- Follow the money. Who benefits and who loses when more freedom is given?

- People throw away all their freedoms to gain a semblance of security. Don't be one of them. Such promises are hollow.

- This is about freedom, not politics.

CONCLUSION

E very day you get to nudge our world either toward or away from farm friendly food. Do not go into a guilt-induced depression over the magnitude of the task. Do not be discouraged over its enormity. You are not responsible for fixing it all.

I think the central question each of us needs to ask ourselves at the end of the day is this: "Today, which food system advanced because of me--farm friendly food or industrial food?"

That is really the only question that matters and the only one you are responsible for. I enjoy a Snickers bar every now and then. And M&Ms won't be hiding from me at a Christmas shindig. And I've even been known to eat a fast food meal--not at McDonald's--once in a blue moon. But the exception of these things is the point.

Don't be so uptight about being true blue through and through that you get ulcers over your diet. This book is not about making you frustrated and depressed.

But each of us, in some way, can affect the ultimate triumph of one of these two food systems. If everyone ate as much candy as I did, it would not even exist in the supermarket. It would exist in confectionary kitchens as cottage industries in individual communities. And it would probably be expensive as a specialty item. That's okay--our culture would probably be a better place if candy were more expensive.

Conclusion

My goal for each of us would be that we would at least think, at least break stride, before patronizing the industrial fare. When we think about the environment, the plight of plants and animals, the nutrition of our families, we have a responsibility to act in accordance with some moral and ethical discernment. None of us will ever be 100 percent consistent. But we can aspire to be 50 percent. Or 60 percent.

Every day thousands of farmers across this land go against their peers, the academic institutions, the farm organizations that receive the media spotlight, and a legion of bureaucrats to produce and process farm friendly food. This food keeps dollars turning in local communities. This food maintains green spaces without government programs and expensive taxpayer-purchased development rights or easements. This food maintains clean water and fresh air for all of us to enjoy. This food protects our watersheds, viewscapes, and natural resources.

Farm friendly food respects the wisdom of the Creator's DNA, honors the information in the mind of an earthworm, and appreciates the beauty of hogs in their rooting heaven. This food values bioregions, social structure, and wildness. It ponders the environmental and moral footprint of every decision, every activity, every marketing model.

You, as a food buyer, have the distinct privilege of proactively participating in shaping the world your children will inherit. Will it be a world of soilent green, of cloned cookie-cutter sameness? Or will it be a world resplendent with variety, a veritable panoply of heritage diversity? Will it be a world of rural landscapes shaped by global positioning satellite-steered machines manipulated from a robotic computer console half a continent away? Or will it be a rural landscape blooming with diversity, brimming with dancing children, and blossoming with pasture flowers?

You don't need to wait until Congress is in session to impact what you eat for dinner tonight. You don't need to wait until the next Farm Bill to voice your concerns about the USDA budget. You don't need to picket the next World Trade Organization talks in order to affect who wins and loses in this great quest for the global food dollar.

Right here, right now, you can do something. You can vote with your food dollar. You can go to a farmers' market. You can contact your state's alternative farming association. You can pick a day next week to

125

fix an entire meal from scratch from something local. You've just read lots of things you can do.

But just like any action, the most critical thing is that you do *something*. Today. At least this week. Otherwise, you will have been given knowledge that requires action, and refused to act. That is worse than ignorance. A whole world, a wonder world, exists outside of Wal-Mart. And although it's not a sin to go there, it may be a sin to go frequently.

If you are a person of conviction, a person of action, you will begin with one step, a second step, then a third. New habits are formed one tiny change at a time. A year from now you'll look back and wonder how you ever tolerated that factory fare. Your children won't eat eggs from the store because they don't taste any good. You'll be emotionally and spiritually uplifted, knowing your food buying has encouraged farm friendly food.

You *are* a partner with your farmers. And we farmers know we're partners with you--we can't do it without your participation. Together we are a team.

To all caring food buyers, I honor you. To all farm friendly food producers, I honor you. We must be committed, focused, and persistent if we are to see farm friendly food triumph. It can. It's up to us. Let's keep on keeping on.

Appendix - Resources

The Weston A. Price Foundation
PMB 106-380, 4200 Wisconsin Avenue, NW
Washington, DC 20016
Phone: (202)333-HEAL
www.westonaprice.org

Eatwild
29428 129th Ave SW
Vashon WA 98070
www.eatwild.com

Eating Fresh Publications
16 Seminary Av.
Hopewell, NJ 08525
(609) 466-1700
www.eatingfresh.com

Virginia Independent Consumers and Farmers Association
P.O. Box 915
Charlottesville, Va. 22902-0915
www.vicfa.net

Chef's Collaborative
262 Beacon Street
Boston, MA 02116
(617) 236-5200
www.chefscollaborative.org

Slow Food U.S.A. National Office
434 Broadway, 6th Floor
New York, NY 10013
(212) 965-5640
www.slowfoodusa.org

North American Farmers' Direct Marketing Association
62 Whiteloaf Rd.
Southampton, MA 01073
(413) 529-0386
www.nafdma.com

USDA Farmer Direct Marketing
Directory of Farmers' Markets in the United States
www.ams.usda.gov/directmarketing/

Index

How to order additional copies of this book

Bring your customers up to speed

Alternative farm marketers can purchase box-lot volumes of this book at half the retail price. Deepen your patron loyalty by offering this guide at cost or free. It may be the best investment in your customers you will ever make. An informed customer is a loyal customer.

For bulk orders of this book, contact:

Polyface, Inc.
43 Pure Meadows Lane
Swoope, VA 24479
Phone: (540) 885-3590 or (540) 887-8194
FAX: (540) 885-5888

For single copies, contact your local bookstore or order via www.amazon.com.